Coffee Break Python Workbook

127 Python Puzzles to Push You from Zero to Hero in Your Coffee Breaks

Christian Mayer, Lukas Rieger, and Zohaib Riaz

January 23, 2020

A puzzle a day to learn, code, and play.

Contents

Contents   ii

1 Introduction   1

2 A Case for Puzzle-based Learning   4
    2.1 Overcome the Knowledge Gap   5
    2.2 Embrace the Eureka Moment   6
    2.3 Divide and Conquer   7
    2.4 Improve From Immediate Feedback . . .   8
    2.5 Measure Your Skills   9
    2.6 Individualized Learning   11
    2.7 Small is Beautiful   11
    2.8 Active Beats Passive Learning   13
    2.9 Make Code a First-class Citizen   15
    2.10 What You See is All There is   17

CONTENTS   iii

3 Elo   **19**
   3.1   How to Use This Book   19
   3.2   How to Test and Train Your Skills? . . .   21
   3.3   What Can This Book Do For You? . . .   25

4 A Quick Overview of the Python Language   **29**
   4.1   Keywords 30
   4.2   Basic Data Types 33
   4.3   Complex Data Types   36
   4.4   Classes 41
   4.5   Functions and Tricks 44

5 Puzzles: Basic to Scholar   **48**
   5.1   Printing values 48
   5.2   Basics of variables. 50
   5.3   Getting started with strings 51
   5.4   Types of variables I 52
   5.5   Types of Variables II   53
   5.6   Minimum   54
   5.7   String Concatenation 55
   5.8   Line Breaks I   56
   5.9   Line Breaks II 57
   5.10 List Length   58
   5.11 Comparison Operators I   59
   5.12 Comparison Operators II   60
   5.13 Multiple Initializations 61

6 Puzzles: Scholar to Intermediate   **63**

6.1	Maximum	63
6.2	Memory addresses	64
6.3	Swapping Values	65
6.4	The Boolean Operator AND	67
6.5	The Boolean Operator OR	69
6.6	Boolean Operators	71
6.7	Arithmetic Expressions	73
6.8	Integer Division and Modulo	75
6.9	Building Strings	77
6.10	The `len()` Function	78
6.11	String Indices	79
6.12	The upper() Function	80
6.13	The lower() Function	81
6.14	Somebody Is Shouting	82
6.15	Counting Characters	83
6.16	String Lengths	84
6.17	Finding Characters in Strings	85
6.18	Not Finding Characters in Strings	86
6.19	Counting Letters	87
6.20	Min() and Max() of a String	88
6.21	Reversed Strings	89
6.22	String Equality	90
6.23	Slicing I	92
6.24	Slicing II	93
6.25	Slicing III	94
6.26	Slicing IV	95
6.27	Slicing V	96

CONTENTS v

6.28 Memory Addresses and Slicing 97
6.29 Accessing List Items I 98
6.30 Accessing List Items II 100
6.31 List as Stack 101
6.32 More String Operations 102
6.33 Checking for Substrings 103
6.34 Stripping String Boundaries 104
6.35 Strings: Stripping vs. Replacement . . . 105
6.36 Gluing Strings Together 106
6.37 The Copy Operation 107
6.38 Growing List Contents I 109
6.39 Growing List Contents II 110
6.40 List Operations I 112
6.41 List Operations II 113
6.42 List Operations III 114
6.43 List Operations IV 115
6.44 List Operations V 116
6.45 List Operations VI 116
6.46 List Operations VII 117
6.47 List Operations VIII 118
6.48 List Operations IX 119
6.49 List Operations X 120
6.50 Lists and the Range Function I 121
6.51 Lists and the Range Function II 122
6.52 Lists and the Range Function III . . . 123
6.53 Python's Multiple Assignment I 124
6.54 Slice Assignments 125

6.55	Strings and Lists II	126
6.56	String Comparisons	127
6.57	From Booleans to Strings	128
6.58	Boolean Trickery I	129
6.59	Boolean Trickery II	130
6.60	Boolean Trickery III	131
6.61	Looping over Ranges	132
6.62	Reversed Loops	134
6.63	Boolean Trickery IV	135
6.64	Lists and Memory Addresses	136
6.65	List Objects	137
6.66	Boolean Tricks	138
6.67	Complex Numbers	139
6.68	Tuples	140
6.69	Multiple Assignments	141
6.70	Boolean Integer Conversion	142
6.71	The `any()` Function	143
6.72	The `sum()` Function	145
6.73	Accessing Complex Numbers	147
6.74	Tuple Confusion	149
6.75	Understanding While ... Else (1/3) . . .	150
6.76	Understanding While ... Else (2/3) . . .	152
6.77	Understanding While ... Else (3/3) . . .	154
6.78	Basic Arithmetic	156
6.79	Dictionary	158
6.80	Dictionary of Dictionaries	160
6.81	Reverse Dictionary Index	162

	6.82 Default Arguments	164
7	**Puzzles: Intermediate to Professional**	**167**
	7.1 Building Strings II	167
	7.2 String: Slicing and Indexing	169
	7.3 Built-in Python Operations	170
	7.4 Strings and Lists I	171
	7.5 Formatting Printouts	173
	7.6 Floating Point Comparisons	174
	7.7 Python's Multiple Assignment II	176
	7.8 The Not-So-Obvious Case	178
	7.9 Rounding Values	179
	7.10 Initializing Integers	181
	7.11 Basic Typing	182
	7.12 Short Circuiting	183
	7.13 While Arithmetic	186
	7.14 The Lambda Function	187
	7.15 Zip	188
	7.16 Basic Filtering	190
	7.17 List Comprehension	193
	7.18 Encryption by Obfuscation	194
	7.19 String Dictionary	197
	7.20 Functions are Objects	198
	7.21 Dictionary of Dictionaries	200
	7.22 Sorting Dictionary Keys	202
	7.23 Pythonic Loop Iteration	204
	7.24 Filtering with List Comprehension	206
	7.25 Aggregating with List Comprehension . .	208

7.26	Maximum of Tuples	210
7.27	The Key Argument	213
7.28	Puzzle 123	214
7.29	Set Operations (1/2)	216
7.30	Set Operations (2/2)	217
7.31	Recursive Algorithm	219
7.32	Fibonacci	222

8 Final Remarks — 226
- Your skill level — 226
- Where to go from here? — 227

9 50 Bonus Workouts — 235

9.1	Arithmetic	235
9.2	Whitespace	236
9.3	Modulo	237
9.4	Tuple	238
9.5	Dictionary	239
9.6	Asterisk	240
9.7	Slicing 1	241
9.8	Slicing 2	242
9.9	Nested Loop	243
9.10	List Arithmetic	244
9.11	Exception	245
9.12	Insert	246
9.13	Sorted Dictionary	247
9.14	Default	248
9.15	Keyword Argument	249

9.16 Global	250
9.17 Flow 1	251
9.18 Flow 2	252
9.19 Enumerate	253
9.20 Reverse	254
9.21 Hierarchical Functions	255
9.22 Sorting++	256
9.23 Indexing	257
9.24 Count	258
9.25 Power	259
9.26 Lambda	260
9.27 Recursion	261
9.28 Kwargs	262
9.29 Dictionary Magic	263
9.30 Sort Key	264
9.31 Print	265
9.32 Logic	266
9.33 Argument Confusion	267
9.34 Pass	268
9.35 List Magic	269
9.36 Zipzip	270
9.37 Comprehension	271
9.38 Slice Extend	272
9.39 Max	273
9.40 Zip	274
9.41 Unpack	275
9.42 Minimax	276

9.43 Sort 277
9.44 Tuple List 278
9.45 While 279
9.46 String Logic 280
9.47 Unorthodox Dict 281
9.48 Count 282
9.49 Cut 283
9.50 End 284

— 1 —
Introduction

The main driver for mastery is neither a character trait nor talent. Mastery comes from intense, structured training. The author Malcolm Gladwell formulated the famous rule of 10,000 hours after collecting research from various fields such as psychology and neurological science.[1] The rule states that if you have average talent, you will reach mastery in any discipline after investing approximately 10,000 hours of intense training. Bill Gates, the founder of Microsoft, reached mastery at a young age as a result of coding for more than 10,000 hours. He was committed and passionate about coding and worked long nights to develop his skills. He was anything but an overnight success.

If you are reading this book, you are an aspiring coder

---

[1] Malcolm Gladwell *Outliers: The Story of Success*

and seek ways to advance your coding skills. Nurturing your ambition to learn will pay dividends to you and your family for as long as you live. It will make you a respectable member of society. Plus you provide value to different parts of society such as information technology, automation, and digitization. Ultimately, it will give you confidence. So, keeping your ambition to learn is the one thing you must place above all else.

The *Coffee Break Python Workbook* is the fourth book in the series.[2] In a way, it's an extension of its predecessor *Coffee Break Python*[3]—but with 127 brand-new code puzzles teaching new Python concepts, it stands on its own.

This book aims to be a stepping stone on your path to becoming a Python master. It helps you to learn faster by using the principles of good teaching. It contains 15-25 hours of Python training using one of the most efficient learning techniques: *practice testing*. This technique is guaranteed to improve your ability to read, write, and understand Python source code.

The idea is that you solve code puzzles. They start simple and become more and more complex as you read the book. In essence, you play the Python interpreter and

---

[2]The third book is more advanced. It's about NumPy, Python's library for data science and numerical computation: `https://blog.finxter.com/coffee-break-numpy/`

[3]`https://blog.finxter.com/coffee-break-python/`

compute the output of each code snippet in your head. Then you check whether you were right. Using the accompanying feedback and explanations, you will adapt and improve your coding skills over time. To make this idea a reality, I developed the online coding academy `Finxter.com`. The next section explains the advantages of the Finxter method of puzzle-based learning. If you already know about the benefits of puzzle-based learning from previous books, and you want to dive right into the puzzles, you can skip the following chapter and start at Chapter 5.

— 2 —
A Case for Puzzle-based Learning

> **Definition:** A *code puzzle* is an educational snippet of source code that teaches a single computer science concept by activating the learner's curiosity and involving them in the learning process.

Before diving into practical puzzle-solving, let's first study 10 reasons why puzzle-based learning accelerates your learning speed and improves retention of the learned material. There is robust evidence in psychological science for each of these reasons. Yet, none of the existing coding books lift code puzzles to being first-class citizens. Instead, they mostly focus on one-directional teaching. This book attempts to change that. In brief, the 10 reasons for puzzle-based learning are:

1. Overcome the Knowledge Gap (Section 2.1)
2. Embrace the Eureka Moment (Section 2.2)
3. Divide and Conquer (Section 2.3)
4. Improve From Immediate Feedback (Section 2.4)
5. Measure Your Skills (Section 2.5)
6. Individualized Learning (Section 2.6)
7. Small is Beautiful (Section 2.7)
8. Active Beats Passive Learning (Section 2.8)
9. Make Source Code a First-class Citizen (Section 2.9)
10. What You See is All There is (Section 2.10)

2.1 Overcome the Knowledge Gap

The great teacher Socrates delivered complex knowledge by asking a sequence of questions. Each question built on answers to previous questions provided by the student. This teaching is more than 2400 years old and is still in widespread use today. A good teacher opens a gap between their knowledge and the learner's. The knowledge gap makes the learner realize that they do not know the answer to a burning question. This creates tension in the learner's mind. To close this gap, the learner waits for the missing piece of knowledge from the teacher. Better yet, the learner starts developing their own answers. The learner *craves knowledge*.

Code puzzles open an immediate knowledge gap. When you first look at the code, you do not understand the meaning of the puzzle. The puzzle's semantics are hidden. But only you can transform the unsolved puzzle into a solved one.

The problem of many teachers is that they open a knowledge gap that is too large. The learner feels frustrated because they cannot cross this gap. *Rated* code puzzles solve this problem because, by design, they are not too great a challenge. You must stretch yourself to solve them, but you can do it if you go all-out.

2.2 Embrace the Eureka Moment

Humans are unique because of their ability to learn. Fast and thorough learning has always increased our chances of survival. Thus, evolution created a brilliant biological reaction to reinforce learning in your body. Your brain is wired to seek new information; it is wired to always process data, to always learn.

Did you ever feel the sudden burst of happiness after experiencing a eureka moment? Your brain releases endorphins, the moment you close a knowledge gap. The instant gratification from learning is highly addictive and this addiction makes you smarter. Solving puzzles gives your brain instant gratification. Easy puzzles lead to harder puzzles, which open large knowledge gaps. Each one you solve, shortens the knowledge gap and you learn in the process.

2.3 Divide and Conquer

Learning to code is a complex task. You must learn a myriad of new concepts and language features. Many aspiring coders are overwhelmed by this complexity. So they seek a clear path to mastery.

As any productivity expert will tell you: break a big goal into a series of smaller steps. Finishing each tiny step brings you one step closer to your big goal. *Divide and conquer* makes you feel in control and takes you one step closer to mastery.

Code puzzles do this for you. They break up the huge task of learning to code into a series of smaller steps. You experience laser focus on one learning task at a time such as *recursion*, the *for loop*, or *keyword arguments*. Each puzzle is a step toward your bigger goal of mastering computer science. Keep solving puzzles and you keep improving your skills.

2.4 Improve From Immediate Feedback

As a child, you learned to walk by trial and error—try, receive feedback, adapt, and repeat. Unconsciously, you will minimize negative and maximize positive feedback. You avoid falling because it hurts, and you seek the approval of your parents. To learn anything, you need feedback so that you can adapt your actions.

However, an excellent learning environment provides you not just with feedback but with *immediate* feedback for your actions. If you were to slap your friend each time he lit a cigarette—a not overly drastic measure to save his life—he would quickly stop smoking. Puzzle-based learning with this book offers you an environment with immediate feedback. This makes learning to code easy and fast. Over time, your brain will absorb the meaning of a code snippet quicker and with higher precision. Learning this skill will take you to the top 10% of all coders.

2.5 Measure Your Skills

Think about an experienced Python programmer you know. How good are their Python skills compared to yours? On a scale from your grandmother to Bill Gates, where is that person and where are you? These questions are difficult to answer because there is no simple way to measure the skill level of a programmer. This creates a problem for your learning progress. The concept of being a good programmer has become fuzzy and diluted. What you can't measure, you can't improve.

So what should be your measurable goal when learning to program? To answer this, let's travel briefly to the world of chess. This sport provides an excellent learning environment for aspiring players. Every player has an Elo rating number that measures their skill level. You get an Elo rating when playing against other players—if you win, your Elo rating increases. Victories against stronger players lead to a higher increase in the Elo rating. Every ambitious chess player simply focuses on one thing: increasing their Elo rating. The ones that manage to push their Elo rating very high, earn grandmaster titles. They become respected among chess players and in the outside world.

Every chess player dreams of being a grandmaster. The goal is as measurable as it can be: reaching an Elo of 2400 and master level (see Section 3). Thus, chess is a great learning environment as every player is always aware of their skill level. A player can measure how their decisions and habits impact their Elo number. Do they improve when sleeping enough before important games? When training opening variants? When solving chess puzzles? What you can measure, you can improve.

The main idea of this book and the associated learning app `Finxter.com` is to transfer this method of measuring skills from the chess world to programming. Suppose you want to learn Python. The Finxter website assigns you a rating that reflects your coding skills. Every Python puzzle has a rating number according to its difficulty level. You 'play' against a puzzle at your difficulty level. The puzzle and you will have a similar Elo rating so that your learning is personalized. If you solve the puzzle, your Elo increases and the puzzle's Elo decreases. Otherwise, your Elo decreases and the puzzle's Elo increases. Hence, the Elo ratings of the difficult puzzles increase over time. But only learners with high Elo ratings will see them. This self-organizing system ensures that you are always challenged but not overwhelmed. Plus you constantly receive feedback about how good your skills are in comparison to others. You always know exactly where you stand on your path to mastery.

2.6 Individualized Learning

Today, the education system is built around the idea of classes and courses. In these environments, all students consume the same learning material from the same teacher applying the same teaching methods.

In the digital era, however, computer servers and intelligent machines provide individualized learning with ease. Puzzle-based learning is a perfect example of automated, individualized learning. The ideal puzzle stretches the student's abilities and is neither boring nor overwhelming. Finding the perfect learning material for each learner is an important and challenging problem. Finxter uses a simple but effective solution to solve this problem: the Elo rating system. The student solves puzzles at their skill level. This book and the book's web backend Finxter push teaching towards individualized learning.

2.7 Small is Beautiful

The 21st century has seen the rise of microcontent. Microcontent is a short and accessible piece of information such as the weather forecast, a news headline, or a cat video. Social media giants like Facebook and Twitter offer a stream of never-ending microcontent. Microcontent has many benefits: the consumer stays engaged and it is easily digestible in a short amount of time. Each piece of microcontent pushes your knowledge horizon a bit further. Today, millions of people are addicted to microcontent.

However, this addiction will become a problem. The computer science professor, Cal Newport, shows in his book *Deep Work* that modern society values deep work more than shallow work. Deep work is a high-value activity that needs intense focus and skill. Examples of deep work are programming, writing, or researching. On the other hand, shallow work is a low-value activity that can be done by anybody e.g., posting cat videos to social media. The demand for deep work has grown with the rise of the information society. At the same time, the supply has stayed constant or decreased. One reason for this is the addictiveness of shallow social media. People that see and understand this trend can benefit tremendously. In a free market, the prices of scarce and high-demand resources rise. Because of this, surgeons, lawyers, and software developers earn \$100,000+ per year. Their work cannot easily be replaced or outsourced to unskilled workers. If you can do deep work and focus your attention on a challenging problem, society pays you generously.

What if we could marry the concept of microcontent with deep work? This is the promise of puzzle-based learning. Finxter offers a stream of self-contained microcontent in the form of hundreds of small code puzzles. But instead of just being unrelated nonsense, each puzzle is a tiny stimulus that teaches a coding concept or language feature. Hence, each puzzle pushes your knowledge *in the same direction*.

Puzzle-based learning breaks the big goal of *reach mastery level in Python* into tiny actionable steps: solve and understand one code puzzle per day. A clear path to success.

2.8 Active Beats Passive Learning

Robust scientific evidence shows that active learning doubles students' learning performance. In a study on this matter, test scores of active learners improved by more than a grade compared to their passive learning counterparts.[1] Not using active learning techniques wastes your time and hinders you if you want to reach your full potential. Switching to active learning is a simple tweak that instantly improves your performance.

How does active learning work? Active learning requires the student to interact with the material, rather

---

[1] https://en.wikipedia.org/wiki/Active_learning#Research_evidence

than simply consume it. It is student-centric rather than teacher-centric. Great active learning techniques are asking and answering questions, self-testing, teaching, and summarizing. A popular study shows that one of the best learning techniques is *practice testing*.[2] In this technique, you test your knowledge before you have learned everything. Rather than *learning by doing*, it's *learning by testing*.

The study argues that students must feel safe during these tests. Therefore, the tests must be low-stakes, i.e., students have little to lose. After the test, students get feedback on how well they did. The study shows that practice testing boosts long-term retention by almost a factor of 10. So, solving a daily code puzzle is not just another learning technique—it is one of the best.

Although active learning is twice as effective, most books focus on passive learning. The author delivers information; the student passively consumes the information. Some programming books include active learning elements by adding tests or by asking the reader to try out the code examples. Yet, I've always found this impractical when reading on the train, bus or in bed. If these active elements drop out, learning becomes 100% passive again.

---

[2] `http://journals.sagepub.com/doi/abs/10.1177/1529100612453266`

Fixing this mismatch between research and common practice drove me to write this book about puzzle-based learning. In contrast to other books, this book makes active learning a first-class citizen. Solving code puzzles is an inherent active learning technique. You must figure out the solution yourself for every single puzzle. The teacher is as much in the background as possible—they only explain the correct solution if you couldn't work it out yourself. But before telling you the correct solution, your knowledge gap is already ripped wide open. Thus, you are mentally ready to digest new material.

2.9 Make Code a First-class Citizen

Each chess grandmaster has spent tens of thousands of hours looking at a nearly infinite number of chess positions. Over time, they develop a powerful skill: the intuition of the expert. When presented with a new position, they can name a small number of strong candidate moves within seconds. They operate on a higher level than normal people. For normal people, the position of a single chess piece is one chunk of information. Hence they can only memorize the position of about six chess pieces. But chess grandmasters view a whole position or a sequence of moves as a single chunk of information. This extensive training and experience has burned strong patterns into their biological neural networks. Their brain can hold much more information—a result of the good learning environment they have put themselves in.

Chess exemplifies principles of good learning that are valid in any field you want to master.

First, transform the object you want to learn into a stimulus and then look at that it over and over. In chess, study as many chess positions as you can. In math, read mathematical papers containing theorems and proofs. In coding, expose yourself to lots of code.

Second, seek feedback. Immediate feedback is better than delayed feedback. However, delayed feedback is still better than no feedback at all.

Third, take your time to learn and understand thoroughly. Although it is possible to learn on-the-go, you will cut corners. The person who prepares beforehand always has an edge. In the world of coding, some people recommend learning by coding practical projects and doing nothing more. Chess grandmasters, sports stars, and intelligent machines do not follow this advice. They learn by practicing small parts again and again until they have mastered them. Then they move on to more complex bits.

Puzzle-based learning is code-centric. You will find your-

2.10. WHAT YOU SEE IS ALL THERE IS   17

self staring at the code for a long time until the insight strikes. This creates new synapses in your brain that help you understand, write, and read code fast. Placing code in the center of the learning process means you will develop an intuition as powerful as the experts. *Maximize the learning time you spend looking at code rather than other things.*

2.10 What You See is All There is

My professor of theoretical computer science used to tell us that if we stare long enough at a proof, the meaning will transfer to our brains by osmosis. This fosters deep thinking, a state of mind where learning is more productive. In my experience, his staring method works—but only if the proof contains everything you need to know to solve it. It must be self-contained.

A good code puzzle beyond the most basic level is self-contained. You can solve it by staring at it until your mind follows your eyes, i.e., your mind develops a solution from rational thinking. There is no need to look things up. If you are a great programmer, you will find the solution quickly. If not, it will take more time but you will still find the solution—it is just more challenging.

My gold standard was to design each puzzle such that they are (mostly) self-contained. However, to ensure you learn new concepts, puzzles must introduce new syntactical language elements as well. Even if the syntax in a puzzle challenges you, develop your own solutions based on your imperfect knowledge. This probabilistic thinking opens the knowledge gap and prepares your brain to receive and digest the explained solution. After all, your goal is long-term retention of the material.

— 3 —

The Elo Rating for Python

Pick any sport you've always loved to play. How good are you compared to others? The Elo rating answers this question with surprising accuracy. It assigns a number to each player that represents their skill in the sport. The higher the Elo number, the better the player.

Table 3.1 shows the ranks for each Elo rating level. The table is an opportunity for you to estimate your Python skill level. In the following, I'll describe how you can use this book to test your Python skills.

3.1 How to Use This Book

This book contains 127 code puzzles and explanations to test and train your Python skills. The puzzles start

Elo rating	Rank
2500	World Class
2400-2500	Grandmaster
2300-2400	International Master
2200-2300	Master
2100-2200	National Master
2000-2100	Master Candidate
1900-2000	Authority
1800-1900	Professional
1700-1800	Expert
1600-1700	Experienced Intermediate
1500-1600	Intermediate
1400-1500	Experienced Learner
1300-1400	Learner
1200-1300	Scholar
1100-1200	Autodidact
1000-1100	Beginner
0-1000	Basic Knowledge

Table 3.1: Elo ratings and skill levels.

from beginner-level and become gradually harder. At the end, you will be an intermediate-level coder. The Elo ranges from 987 to 1899 points (between *beginner* and *professional* level in the table). Follow-up books cover more advanced levels. This book is perfect for you if you are between the beginner and intermediate levels. Yet, even experts will improve their speed of code understanding if they follow the outlined strategy.

3.2 How to Test and Train Your Skills?

I recommend solving at least one code puzzle every day, e.g. as you drink your morning coffee. Then spend the rest of your learning time on real projects that matter to you. The puzzles guarantee that your skills will improve over time and the real project brings you results.

To test your Python skills, do the following:

1. Track your Elo rating as you read the book and solve the code puzzles. Write your current Elo rating in the book. Start with an initial rating of 1000 if you are a beginner, 1500 if you are an intermediate, and 2000 if you are an advanced Python programmer. Of course, if you already have an online rating on `finxter.com`, start with that. Fig-

ure 3.2 shows five different examples of how your Elo will change while working through the book. Two factors impact the final rating: how you select your initial rating and how good you perform (the latter being more important).

2. If your solution is correct, add the Elo points given with the puzzle. Otherwise, subtract the points from your current Elo number.

Solve the puzzles sequentially because they build upon each other. Advanced readers can solve them in the sequence they wish—the Elo rating will work just as well.

Use the following training plan to develop a strong learning habit with puzzle-based learning.

1. Choose or create a daily trigger after which you'll solve code puzzles for 10 minutes. For example, decide on your *Coffee Break Python*. Or solve code puzzles as you brush your teeth or sit on the train to work, university, or school.

2. Scan over the puzzle and ask yourself: what is the unique idea of this puzzle?

3. Dive deeply into the code. Try to understand the purpose of each symbol, even if it seems trivial at

3.2. HOW TO TEST AND TRAIN YOUR SKILLS 23

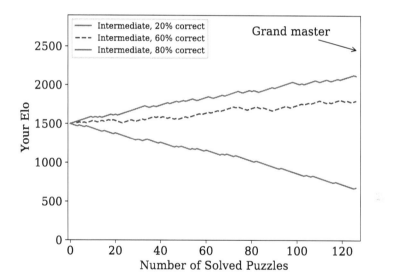

Figure 3.1: This is an example of how your Elo rating could change while working through the 127 puzzles. Your final Elo rating depends on where you started and (to a larger extent) on the percentage of correctly solved puzzles.

first. Avoid being shallow and lazy. Instead, solve each puzzle thoroughly and take your time. It may seem counter intuitive at first but to learn faster, you must take your time and allow yourself to dig deep. There is no shortcut.

4. Stay objective when evaluating your solution—we all tend to lie to ourselves.

5. Look up the solution and read the explanation with care. Do you understand every aspect of the code? Write any questions down that you have and look up the answers later. Or send them to me (`admin@finxter.com`). I will do everything I can to come up with a good explanation.

6. If your solution was 100% correct—including whitespaces, data types, and formatting of the output—you get the Elo points for this puzzle. Otherwise, your solution was wrong and you should subtract Elo points. This rule is strict because code is either right or wrong. If you miss some whitespace in the 'real world', you may get an error. So make sure you don't forget it in training.

As you follow this simple training plan, your ability to quickly understand source code will improve. In the long term, this will have a huge impact on your career, income, and work satisfaction. You do not have to invest much time because the training plan requires only 10–20 minutes per day. But you must be persistent with your effort. If you get off track, get right back on the next day. When you run out of code puzzles, feel free to checkout `Finxter.com`. It has more than 300 handcrafted code puzzles and I regularly publish new ones.

3.3 What Can This Book Do For You?

Before we dive into puzzle-solving, let me address some common misconceptions about this book.

The puzzles are too easy/too hard. This book is for you if you already have some coding experience. Your Python skill level ranges from beginner to intermediate. If you are already an advanced coder, this book is for you too—if you read it differently. Simply measure the time you need to solve the puzzles and limit your solution time to 10–20 seconds. This introduces an additional challenge for solving the puzzles: time pressure. Solving puzzles under time pressure sharpens your rapid code understanding skills even more. Eventually, you will feel that your coding intuition has improved. If the puzzles are too hard, great. Your knowledge gap must be open before you can effectively absorb information. Just take your time to thoroughly understand every bit of new information. Study the cheat sheets in Chapter 4 properly.

Why is this book not conventionally structured by topic? The puzzles are sorted by Elo and not structured by topic. Puzzles with a small Elo rating are easier and more fundamental. Puzzles with a higher Elo rating are harder. To solve them, you need to combine the fundamental lessons from the easier puzzles. Ordering puzzles by difficulty has many advantages one being that you can solve puzzles at your skill level. As you get better, the puzzles get harder. Finally, ordering by complexity allows us to combine many topics in a single puzzle. For example, a Python one-liner may use two topics: list comprehension and lambda functions.

Learning to code is best done via coding projects. I agree but it's only part of the truth. Yes, you can improve your skills by diving into practical projects. But, as in every other discipline, your skills will quickly hit an upper limit. These limits come from a lack of understanding of the basic concepts. You cannot understand high level knowledge without first understanding the basic building blocks. Have you ever used machine learning techniques in your work? Without theoretical foundations, you are doomed. Theory pushes your ceiling upwards and gets rid of the limitations that hold you back.

Abraham Lincoln said: *"Give me six hours to chop down*

3.3. WHAT CAN THIS BOOK DO FOR YOU?

a tree and I will spend the first four sharpening the ax." Do not fool yourself into the belief that *just doing it* is the most effective road to reach any goal. You must constantly sharpen the saw to be successful in any discipline. Learning to code is best done via practical coding *and* investing time into your personal growth. Millions of computer scientists have an academic background. They know that solving hundreds or thousands of toy examples in their studies built a strong foundation.

How am I supposed to solve this puzzle if I do not know the meaning of this specific Python language feature? Guess it! Python is an intuitive language. Think about potential meanings. Solve the puzzle for each of them— a good exercise for your brain. The more you work on the puzzle, even with imperfect knowledge, the better you prepare your brain to absorb the puzzle's explanation.

How does this book interplay with the puzzles at `Finxter.com`*?* My goal is to remove barriers to learning Python. Thus, many puzzles are available for free online. This book is based on some puzzles available at Finxter, but it extends them with more detailed and structured information. Nevertheless, if you don't like reading books, feel free to check out the website.

Anyway, why do some people thrive in their fields and become valued experts while others stagnate? They read books in their field. They increase their value to the marketplace by feeding themselves valuable information. Over time, they have a huge advantage over their peers. They get opportunities to develop themselves even further. They enjoy much higher job satisfaction and life quality. Belonging to the top ten percent of your field yields hundreds of thousands of dollars throughout your career. However, there is a price to pay to unlock the gates of this world: invest in books and personal development. The more time and money you spend on books, the more valuable you become to the marketplace!

The Elo-based rating is not accurate.

The Elo rating will get more accurate the more puzzles you solve. Although only an estimate, your Elo rating is an objective measure to compare your skills with the skills of others. Several Finxter users have reported that the rating is fair and surprisingly accurate. It provides a good indication of where one stands in comparison to other Python coders. If you feel the rating is not accurate, ask yourself whether you are objective. If you think you are, please let me know so that I can improve this book and the Finxter back-end.

— 4 —

A Quick Overview of the Python Language

Before diving into the puzzles, work through the following five cheat sheets. By reading htem, you'll learn 80% of Python's language features in 20% of the time it takes most people. They are definitely worth your time investment.

Read them thoroughly. If you try to understand every single line of code, you will catapult your skills to the next level. Most Python coders don't invest enough time into learning the basics such as the core language features, data types, and language tricks. Be different and absorb the examples in each cheat sheet. Open up your path to become a master coder and join the top ten percent of coders.

You can download all five cheat sheets as concise PDFs. Post them to your wall until you know them by heart: `https://blog.finxter.com/subscribe/`.

4.1 Keywords

All programming languages reserve certain words to have a special meaning. These words are called *keywords*. With keywords, you can issue commands to the compiler or interpreter. They let you tell the computer what to do. Without keywords, the computer would not be able to understand the seemingly random text in your code file. Note that, as keywords are reserved words, you cannot use them as variable names.

The most important Python keywords are:

```
False   True    and       or
not     break   continue  class
def     if      elif      else
for     while   in        is
None    lambda  return
```

The next cheat sheet introduces the most important keywords in Python. In each row, you'll find the keyword, a short description, and an example of its usage.

4.1. KEYWORDS

Keyword	Description	Code example
False, True	Data values from the data type Boolean	`False == (1 > 2)` `True == (2 > 1)`

and, or, not	Logical operators:
	(`x and y`) → both x and y must be True
	(`x or y`) → either x or y must be True
	(`not x`) → x must be false
		`x, y = True, False`
		`(x or y) == True`
		`# True`
		`(x and y) == False`
		`# True`
		`(not y) == True`
		`# True`

break	Ends loop prematurely	`while(True):`
		`    break # no infinite loop`
		`print("hello world")`

continue	Finishes current loop iteration	`while(True):`
		`    continue`
		`    print("43") # dead code`

class
 	
def
	Defines a new class → a real-world concept (object oriented programming)
	
	Defines a new function or class method. For latter, first parameter `self` points to the class object. When calling class method, first parameter is implicit.
		`class Beer:`
		
		`    def __init__(self):`
		`        self.content = 1.0`
		
		`    def drink(self):`
		`        self.content = 0.0`
		
		`# constructor creates class`
		`becks = Beer()`
		
		`# empty beer bottle`
		`becks.drink()`

if, elif,	Conditional program execution: program starts	`x = int(input("your val: "))` `if x > 3: print("Big")`

else	with "if" branch, tries "elif" branches, and finishes with "else" branch (until one evaluates to True).	`elif x == 3: print("Medium")` `else: print("Small")`

for, while	`# For loop`
	`declaration`
	`for i in [0,1,2]:`
	`    print(i)`
		`# While loop - same`
		`semantics`
		`j = 0`
		`while j < 3:`
		`    print(j)`
		`    j = j + 1`

in	Checks whether element is in sequence	`42 in [2, 39, 42] # True`

is	Checks whether both elements point to the same object	`y = x = 3`
		`x is y # True`
		`[3] is [3] # False`

None	Empty value constant	`def f():`
		`    x = 2`
		`f() is None # True`

lambda	Function with no name (anonymous)	`(lambda x: x + 3)(3) #` `returns 6`

return	Terminates function execution and passes the execution flow to the caller. An optional value after the return keyword specifies the result.	`def incrementor(x):`
		`    return x + 1`
		`incrementor(4) # returns 5`

4.2 Basic Data Types

Many programmers call basic data types *primitive data types*. They provide the primitives on which the higher-level concepts are built. A house is built from bricks. Likewise, a complex data type is built from basic data types. I introduce basic data types in the next cheat sheet and complex data types in Section 4.3.

Specifically, the next cheat sheet explains the three most important (classes of) basic data types in Python. First, the *boolean* data type encodes truth values. For example, the expression $42 > 3$ evaluates to `True` and $1 \in \{2, 4, 6\}$ evaluates to `False`. Second, the numerical types *integer*, *float*, and *complex numbers* encode integer values, floating point values and complex values respectively. For example, 41 is an integer value, 41.99 is a float value, and $41.999 + 0.1 * i$ is a complex value (the first part being the real number and the second the imaginary number). Third, the *string* data type encodes textual data. An example of a string value is the Shakespeare quote '`Give every man thy ear, but few thy voice`'.

Data Type + Description	Example

Boolean
The Boolean data type is a truth value, either True or False.
 	
These are important Boolean operators ordered by priority (from highest to lowest):
not x →
"if x is False, then x, else y"
 	
x and y →
"if x is False, then x, else y"
 	
x or y →
"if x is False, then y, else x"
	```x, y = True, False```
	```print(x and not y) # True```
	```print(not x and y or x) # True```
	
	```## All of those evaluate to False```
	```if (None or 0 or 0.0 or '' or []```
	``` or {} or set()):```
	``` print("Dead code")```
	
	```## All of those evaluate to True```
	```if (1 < 2 and 3 > 2 and 2 >=2```
	``` and 1 == 1 and 1 != 0):```
	``` print("True")```

Integer
An integer is a positive or negative number without floating point (e.g. 3).
 	
Float
A float is a positive or negative number with floating point precision (e.g. 3.14159265359).
 	
The '//' operator performs integer division. The result is an integer value that is rounded towards the smaller integer number (e.g. 3 // 2 == 1).
	```## Arithmetic Operations```
	```x, y = 3, 2```
	```print(x + y) # = 5```
	```print(x - y) # = 1```
	```print(x * y) # = 6```
	```print(x / y) # = 1.5```
	```print(x // y) # = 1```
	```print(x % y) # = 1s```
	```print(-x) # = -3```
	```print(abs(-x)) # = 3```
	```print(int(3.9)) # = 3```
	```print(float(3)) # = 3.0```
	```print(x ** y) # = 9```

4.2. BASIC DATA TYPES

String	
Python Strings are sequences of characters. They are immutable which means that you can not alter the characters without creating a new string.	```## Indexing & Slicing
s = "The youngest pope was 11 years old"
print(s[0])   # 'T'
print(s[1:3])   # 'he'
print(s[-3:-1])   # 'ol'
print(s[-3:])   # 'old'
x = s.split() # string array
print(x[-3] + " " + x[-1] + " " + x[2] + "s") # '11 old popes'
``

The four main ways to create strings are the following.
 	
1. Single quotes
`'Yes'`
2. Double quotes
`"Yes"`
3. Triple quotes (multi-line)
`"""Yes`
`We Can"""`
4. String method
`str(5) == '5' # True`
5. Concatenation
`"Ma" + "hatma" #`
`'Mahatma'`
 	
These are whitespace characters in strings.
- Newline `\n`
- Space `\s`
- Tab `\t`
	``## Key String Methods

y = " This is lazy\t\n"
print(y.strip()) # 'This is lazy'
print("DrDre".lower()) # 'drdre'
print("stop".upper()) # 'STOP'
s = "smartphone"
print(s.startswith("smart")) # True
print(s.endswith("phone")) # True
print("another".find("other")) # 2
print("cheat".replace("ch", "m"))
# 'meat'
print(','.join(["F", "B", "I"]))
# 'F,B,I'
print(len("Rumpelstiltskin")) # 15
print("ear" in "earth") # True
``

4.3 Complex Data Types

In the previous section, you learned about basic data types. These are the building blocks for *complex data types*. Think of complex data types as containers—each holds a multitude of (potentially different) data types.

Specifically, the complex data types in this cheat sheet are lists, sets, and dictionaries. A list is an ordered sequence of data values (that can be either basic or complex data types). An example for such an ordered sequence is the list of all US presidents:
`['Washington',`
`'Adams',`
`'Jefferson', ...,`
`'Obama',`
`'Trump'].`

In contrast, a set is an *unordered* sequence of data values:
`{'Trump',`
`'Washington',`
`'Jefferson', ...,`
`'Obama'}.`

Expressing the US presidents as a set loses all ordering information—it's not a sequence anymore. But sets do have an advantage over lists. Retrieving information about particular data values in the set is much faster. For instance, checking whether the string `'Obama'` is in

4.3. COMPLEX DATA TYPES

the set of US presidents is blazingly fast even for large sets. I provide the most important methods and ideas for complex data types in the following cheat sheet.

Complex Data Type + Description	Example
List A container data type that stores a sequence of elements. Unlike strings, lists are mutable: modification possible.	`l = [1, 2, 2]` `print(len(l)) # 3`

Adding elements to a list with append, insert, or list concatenation. The append operation is fastest.	`[1, 2, 2].append(4) # [1, 2, 2, 4]`
	`[1, 2, 4].insert(2,2) # [1, 2, 2, 4]`
	`[1, 2, 2] + [4] # [1, 2, 2, 4]`

Removing elements is slower (find it first).	`[1, 2, 2, 4].remove(1) # [2, 2, 4]`
Reversing the order of elements.	`[1, 2, 3].reverse() # [3, 2, 1]`
Sorting a list Slow for large lists: O(n log n), n list elements.	`[2, 4, 2].sort() # [2, 2, 4]`

Indexing Finds index of the first occurence of an element in the list. Is slow when traversing the whole list.	`[2, 2, 4].index(2)`
	`# index of element 4 is "0"`
	`[2, 2, 4].index(2,1)`
	`# index of el. 2 after pos 1 is "1"`

Stack Python lists can be used intuitively as stack via the two list operations append() and pop().	`stack = [3]`
	`stack.append(42) # [3, 42]`
	`stack.pop() # 42 (stack: [3])`
	`stack.pop() # 3 (stack: [])`

Set	`basket = {'apple', 'eggs',` `            'banana', 'orange'}`

4.3. COMPLEX DATA TYPES

Unordered collection of unique elements (*at-most-once*).	`same = set(['apple', 'eggs',`
	`            'banana', 'orange'])`
	`print(basket == same) # True`

Dictionary
A useful data structure for storing (key, value) pairs.
	`calories = {'apple' : 52,`
	`            'banana' : 89,`
	`            'choco' : 546}`

Reading and writing
Read and write elements by specifying the key within the brackets. Use the keys() and values() functions to access all keys and values of the dictionary.
	`c = calories`
	`print(c['apple'] < c['choco']) # True`
	`c['cappu'] = 74`
	`print(c['banana'] < c['cappu']) # False`
	`print('apple' in c.keys()) # True`
	`print(52 in c.values()) # True`

Dictionary Looping
You can access the (key, value) pairs of a dictionary with the `items()` method.
	`for k, v in calories.items():`
	`    print(k) if v > 500 else None`
	`# 'chocolate'`

Membership operator Check with the keyword `in` whether the set, list, or dictionary contains an element. Set containment is faster than list containment.	`basket = {'apple', 'eggs',`
	`           'banana', 'orange'}`
	`print('eggs' in basket} # True`
	`print('mushroom' in basket} # False`

List and Set Comprehension List comprehension is the concise Python way to create lists. Use brackets plus an expression, followed by a for clause. Close with	`## List comprehension`
	`[('Hi ' + x) for x in ['Alice', 'Bob',`
	`'Pete']]`
	`# ['Hi Alice', 'Hi Bob', 'Hi Pete']`
	`[x * y for x in range(3) for y in`
	`range(3) if x>y]`
	`# [0, 0, 2]`

zero or more for or if clauses. Set comprehension is similar to list comprehension.	``` ## Set comprehension squares = { x**2 for x in [0,2,4] if x < 4 } # {0, 4} ```

4.4 Classes

Object-oriented programming (OOP) is an influential, powerful, and expressive programming paradigm. The programmer thinks in terms of classes and objects. A class is a blueprint for an object. An object contains specific data and provides the functionality specified in the class.

Say, you are programming a game to build, simulate, and grow cities. In object-oriented programming, you would represent all things (buildings, persons, or cars) as objects. For example, each building object stores data such as name, size, and price tag. Additionally, each building provides a defined functionality such as `calculate_monthly_earnings()`. This simplifies the reading and understanding of your code for other programmers. Even more important, you can now easily divide responsibilities between programmers. For example, you code the buildings and your colleague codes the moving cars.

In short, object-oriented programming helps you to write readable code. By learning it, your ability to collaborate with others on complex problems improves. The next cheat sheet introduces the most basic concepts.

Description	Example

Classes
A class encapsulates data and functionality: data as attributes, and functionality as methods. It is a blueprint for creating concrete instances in memory.

	``
	class Dog:
	    """ Blueprint of a dog """
	
	    # class variable
	    # for all instances
	    species = ["canis lupus"]
	
	    def __init__(self, n, c):
	        self.name = n
	        self.state = "sleeping"
	        self.color = c
	
	    def command(self, x):
	        if x == self.name:
	            self.bark(2)
	        elif x == "sit":
	            self.state = "sit"
	        else:
	            self.state = "wag
	                tail"
	
	    def bark(self, freq):
	        for i in range(freq):
	            print(self.name
	                + ": Woof!")
	
	bello = Dog("bello", "black")
	alice = Dog("alice", "white")
	
	print(bello.color) # black
	print(alice.color) # white
	``

Instance You are an instance of the class human. An instance is a concrete implementation of a class: all attributes of an instance have a fixed value. Your hair is blond, brown, or black---but never unspecified. Each instance has its own attributes independent of other instances. Yet, class variables are different. These are data values associated with the class, not the instances. Hence, all instance share the same class variable `species` in the example.	
Self The first argument when defining any method is always the `self` argument. This argument specifies the instance	

4.4. CLASSES

on which you call the method.

`self` gives the Python interpreter the information about the concrete instance. To *define* a method, you use `self` to modify the instance attributes. But to *call* an instance method, you do not need to specify `self`.

```
class Employee():
    pass
employee = Employee()
employee.salary = 122000
employee.firstname = "alice"
employee.lastname =
"wonderland"

print(employee.firstname +
" " + employee.lastname +
" $" + str(employee.salary))
# alice wonderland $122000
```

```
bello.bark(1) # bello: Woof!

alice.command("sit")
print("alice: " +
alice.state)
# alice: sit

bello.command("no")
print("bello: " +
bello.state)
# bello: wag tail

alice.command("alice")
# alice: Woof!
# alice: Woof!

bello.species += ["wulf"]
print(len(bello.species)
    == len(alice.species))
# True (!)
```

4.5 Functions and Tricks

Python is full of extra tricks and special functionality. Learning these tricks makes you more efficient and productive. But more importantly, these tricks make programming easy and fun. In the next cheat sheet, I show you the most important ones.

4.5. FUNCTIONS AND TRICKS

ADVANCED FUNCTIONS

`map(func, iter)`
Executes the function on all elements of the iterable. Example:
`list(map(lambda x: x[0], ['red', 'green', 'blue']))`
`# Result: ['r', 'g', 'b']`

`map(func, i1, ..., ik)`
Executes the function on all k elements of the k iterables. Example:
`list(map(lambda x, y: str(x) + ' ' + y + 's' , [0, 2, 2],`
`['apple', 'orange', 'banana']))`
`# Result: ['0 apples', '2 oranges', '2 bananas']`

`string.join(iter)`
Concatenates iterable elements separated by `string`. Example:
`' marries '.join(list(['Alice', 'Bob']))`
`# Result: 'Alice marries Bob'`

`filter(func, iterable)`
Filters out elements in iterable for which function returns False (or 0). Example:
`list(filter(lambda x: True if x>17 else False, [1, 15, 17, 18]))  # Result: [18]`

`string.strip()`
Removes leading and trailing whitespaces of string. Example:
`print("\n    \t  42   \t ".strip()) # Result: 42`

`sorted(iter)`
Sorts iterable in ascending order. Example:
`sorted([8, 3, 2, 42, 5]) # Result: [2, 3, 5, 8, 42]`

`sorted(iter, key=key)`
Sorts according to the key function in ascending order. Example:
`sorted([8, 3, 2, 42, 5], key=lambda x: 0 if x==42 else x)`
`# [42, 2, 3, 5, 8]`

`help(func)` Returns documentation of func. Example:

`help(str.upper())` # Result: '... to uppercase.'

`zip(i1, i2, ...)`
Groups the i-th elements of iterators i1, i2, ... together. Example:
`list(zip(['Alice', 'Anna'], ['Bob', 'Jon', 'Frank']))`
`# Result: [('Alice', 'Bob'), ('Anna', 'Jon')]`

Unzip
Equal to: 1) unpack the zipped list, 2) zip the result. Example:
`list(zip(*[('Alice', 'Bob'), ('Anna', 'Jon')]`
`# Result: [('Alice', 'Anna'), ('Bob', 'Jon')]`

`enumerate(iter)`
Assigns a counter value to each element of the iterable. Example:
`list(enumerate(['Alice', 'Bob', 'Jon']))`
`# Result: [(0, 'Alice'), (1, 'Bob'), (2, 'Jon')]`

TRICKS
python -m http.server <P> Want to share files between your PC and your phone? Run this command in your PC's shell. <P> is any port number between 0–65535. Type < IP address of PC>:<P> in the phone's browser. Now, you can browse the files in the PC's directory.
Read comic `import antigravity` Opens the comic series xkcd in your web browser

Zen of Python
`import this`
`'...Beautiful is better than ugly. Explicit is ...'`

Swapping variables
This is a breeze in Python. No offense, Java! Example:
`a, b = 'Jane', 'Alice'`
`a, b = b, a`
`# Result: a = 'Alice', b = 'Jane'`

4.5. FUNCTIONS AND TRICKS

Unpacking arguments
Use a sequence as function arguments via asterisk operator *. Use a dictionary (key, value) via double asterisk operator **. Example:
```
def f(x, y, z):
    return x + y * z
f(*[1, 3, 4]) # 13
f(**{'z' : 4, 'x' : 1, 'y' : 3}) # 13
```

Extended Unpacking
Use unpacking for multiple assignment feature in Python. Example:
```
a, *b = [1, 2, 3, 4, 5]
# Result: a = 1, b = [2, 3, 4, 5]
```

Merge two dictionaries
Use unpacking to merge two dictionaries into a single one. Example:
```
x={'Alice' : 18}
y={'Bob' : 27, 'Ann' : 22}
z = {**x,**y}
# Result: z = {'Alice': 18, 'Bob': 27, 'Ann': 22}
```

— 5 —

Python Puzzles: From *Basic Knowledge* to *Scholar* Level

Let's dive into the beginner-level puzzles with Elo rating below `1300`. The solution for each puzzle is on the page after it, so you won't be tempted to cheat and look at the solution! Also, there's some whitespace for notes immediately after each one.

5.1 Printing values

```
# Elo 987

a = 20
print(a)
```

5.1. PRINTING VALUES

What's the output of this code snippet?
Correct: +10 Elo points / Wrong: -10 Elo points

Variable a is initialized with the integer value 20. The statement print(a) prints the value 20 to the screen. Thus, the output is 20.

5.2 Basics of variables

```
# Elo 1023

a = 20
b = 11
c = a - b

print(c)
```

What's the output of this code snippet?
Correct: +10 Elo points / Wrong: -10 Elo points

5.3. GETTING STARTED WITH STRINGS 51

There are three variables a, b, and c. The first two variables hold integer values 20 and 11. The variable c contains the difference of a and b, i.e., 20 - 11 = 9. So, the output of printing c to the screen is 9.

5.3 Getting started with strings

```
# Elo 991

my_string = 'abc'
print(my_string)
```

What's the output of this code snippet?
Correct: +10 Elo points / Wrong: -10 Elo points

In this puzzle, we define a string 'abc' using single quote notation ('...'). A string is a sequence of characters and it represents text.

When we call `print()` on a string, the text itself appears in the shell, i.e., abc.

5.4 Types of variables I

```
# Elo 1189

a = 2
print(type(a))
```

What's the output of this code snippet?
Correct: +10 Elo points / Wrong: -10 Elo points

5.5. TYPES OF VARIABLES II

In this puzzle, we assign the value 2 to variable `a` and print its data type.

Python automatically assigns a `data type` to every variable. Because `a` is an integer, the type printed to the shell is `<class 'int'>`.

5.5 Types of Variables II

```
# Elo 1198

x = True
print(type(x))
```

What's the output of this code snippet?
Correct: +10 Elo points / Wrong: -10 Elo points

We set variable `x` to the Boolean value `True`. Hence, the output is `<class 'bool'>`.

5.6 Minimum

```
# Elo 1245

print(min([1, 2, 3, -4]))
```

What's the output of this code snippet?
Correct: +10 Elo points / Wrong: -10 Elo points

5.7. STRING CONCATENATION

We pass a list of integer values to the built-in `min()` function. This returns the smallest element of the list. Thus, it's the integer -4.

5.7 String Concatenation

```
# Elo 1111

first_str = 'Hello'
second_str = " world!"

str_ = first_str + second_str

print(str_)
```

What's the output of this code snippet?
Correct: +10 Elo points / Wrong: -10 Elo points

This puzzle defines strings in two different ways: single quotes and double quotes. The first string is set to `'Hello'` and the second to `'' world!''`.

After defining the two strings, we join them together (concatenate them) and store the result in the variable `str_`.

Note that our variable has a trailing underscore. This is often used if the variable name would *shadow* another already defined name. The name `str` is already used for Python's built-in function `str()` and converts each object to its textual representation. The trailing underscore ensures we don't overwrite this important built-in function.

Thus, the result is `Hello world!`.

5.8 Line Breaks I

```
# Elo 1298
```

```
my_str = 'Hello\nworld\nhow\nare you?'
print(my_str)
```

What's the output of this code snippet?
Correct: +10 Elo points / Wrong: -10 Elo points

5.9. LINE BREAKS II

This puzzle defines a string with multiple '\n' characters. This is the so-called *new line* character which, not surprisingly, adds a new line to the textual representation. Hence, the result is:

```
Hello
world
how
are you?
```

5.9 Line Breaks II

```
# Elo 1270

my_str = '''Hello
world
how are
you?'''

print(my_str)
```

What's the output of this code snippet?
Correct: +10 Elo points / Wrong: -10 Elo points

58   CHAPTER 5.   PUZZLES: BASIC TO SCHOLAR

This puzzle does the same as the puzzle before but with one difference: instead of encoding the new line using `'\n'`, we define a multi-line string using triple quote notation.

The result is (again):

```
Hello
world
how
are you?
```

5.10   List Length

```
# Elo 1281

my_list = [1, 2, 3, 4, 5]
print(len(my_list))
```

What's the output of this code snippet?
Correct: +10 Elo points / Wrong: -10 Elo points

5.11. COMPARISON OPERATORS I 59

This puzzle creates a list and calculates its length (`len`). For a list, its length is the same as the number of elements in it. There are five numbers, so the result is 5.

5.11 Comparison Operators I

```
# Elo 1112

bool_var = 1 == 1
print(bool_var)
```

What's the output of this code snippet?
Correct: +10 Elo points / Wrong: -10 Elo points

We define the Boolean value `bool_var` as the result of the expression `1==1`. Since the values on either side of the expression are the same, the result is the Boolean value `True`. Hence, the result of the puzzle is: `True`.

5.12 Comparison Operators II

 # Elo 1194

```
bool_var = 1 > 2
print(bool_var)
```

What's the output of this code snippet?
Correct: +10 Elo points / Wrong: -10 Elo points

Similar to the previous puzzle, the variable `bool_var` stores the result of a Boolean expression, this time 1 > 2. Obviously, the result is `False` because 1 is not larger than 2.

5.13 Multiple Initializations

```
# Elo 1297

a = b = c = 1
print(b)
```

What's the output of this code snippet?
Correct: +10 Elo points / Wrong: -10 Elo points

This puzzle uses a concise way of initializing multiple variables at the same time.

The concept of *naming* explains what is going on here: we create a new integer object `1` in memory (on the far right of the first line). Then, we create three names `a`, `b` and `c` and point these names to the same integer object `1`. Although the name may be different, the value these names refer to is the same. Roughly speaking, your colleagues, friends and family may call you different names—but they refer to you in all cases. This view on naming in Python is very important to understand for many advanced language features.

Thus, the result is `1`.

— 6 —

Python Puzzles: From *Scholar* to *Intermediate* Level

Next, you'll have a harder time with puzzles ranging from Elo 1300 to Elo 1600.

6.1 Maximum

```
# Elo 1401

print(max([3+2, 5*2, 12/3]))
```

What's the output of this code snippet?
Correct: +10 Elo points / Wrong: -10 Elo points

In this puzzle, we pass a list of arithmetic expressions to the `max()` function. After evaluating these expressions, the `max()` function returns the greatest value from the list. In our case, the list looks like: [5, 10, 4.0]. Hence, this code prints 10.

6.2 Memory addresses

```
# Elo 1278

question = 'What is the answer?'
answer = 42

question = answer

print(id(question)==id(answer))
```

What's the output of this code snippet?
Correct: +10 Elo points / Wrong: -10 Elo points

The variable `question` is a string with the value `'What is the answer?'`.

The variable `answer` is an integer with the value `42`.

After setting `question = answer`, the variable `question` now refers to variable `answer` which is the integer `42`.

The `id()` function returns the memory address of a Python object. No two objects in memory have the same id if they refer to different things—that's guaranteed.

In this case, both variables `question` and `answer` refer to the same object in memory, so the result is `True`.

6.3 Swapping Values

```
# Elo 1321

a = 5
b = 'my string'

tmp = a
a = b
b = tmp

print(a)
print(b)
```

What's the output of this code snippet?

Correct: +10 Elo points / Wrong: -10 Elo points

6.4. THE BOOLEAN OPERATOR AND

This puzzle defines an integer variable a and a string variable b.

The goal of the puzzle is to swap the values of a and b. To achieve this, we create a new variable tmp that takes the same value as a. Next, we overwrite the value of a to refer to b, i.e., the string value 'my string'.

Note that we have not lost the old reference of a because we stored it in the temporary variable tmp.

Finally, we point b to the original value of a using the temporarily saved value in the variable tmp.

Note that there's a much shorter way of swapping two variables in Python:

```
a, b = b, a
```

This achieves the same result but in a much more concise way. Nevertheless, it does no harm to know this less concise pattern because many coders from other programming languages, such as Java, will use it.

As the two variables are swapped, the final value of a is 'my string' and b is 5.

6.4 The Boolean Operator AND

 # Elo 1432

```
t1 = True
t2 = True
f1 = False
f2 = False

and_result = t1 and t2
print(and_result)

and_result = t1 and f1
print(and_result)

and_result = f1 and f2
print(and_result)

and_result = f1 and t2
print(and_result)
```

What's the output of this code snippet?
Correct: +10 Elo points / Wrong: -10 Elo points

6.5. THE BOOLEAN OPERATOR OR 69

Here, we have four variables `t1, t2, f1, f2`. The variables `t*` are `True` and the variables `f*` are `False`.

The puzzle performs the Boolean `and` operation on all combinations of these four variables.

The `and` operation is `True` if and only if both operands are `True`. Hence, the result is:

True
False
False
False

6.5 The Boolean Operator OR

```
# Elo 1417

t1 = True
t2 = True
f1 = False
f2 = False

or_result = t1 or t2
print(or_result)

or_result = t1 or f1
print(or_result)
```

```
or_result = f2 or t2
print(or_result)

or_result = f1 or f2
print(or_result)
```

What's the output of this code snippet?
Correct: +10 Elo points / Wrong: -10 Elo points

6.6. BOOLEAN OPERATORS

Like in the previous puzzle, the variables t1, t2, f1, f2 are Boolean values True for t* and False for f*.

In contrast to the previous puzzle, this one performs logical or operations on all combinations of these Boolean values.

The logical or operation returns True if at least one of the operands is True. This is the case for all but the last instance. So the result is:

```
True
True
True
False
```

6.6 Boolean Operators

```
# Elo 1476

t1 = 5 + 2 == 7
f1 = 2 - 1 > 3

r = t1 or False
r = r and True and f1

print(r)
```

What's the output of this code snippet?

CHAPTER 6. PUZZLES: SCHOLAR TO INTERMEDIATE

Correct: +10 Elo points / Wrong: -10 Elo points

Variables `t1` and `f1` hold the results of two simple expressions. The first expression evaluates to `True` and the second to `False`.

Be careful not to evaluate the Boolean statement first (for example: `5 + (2 == 7)`). Instead, the arithmetic operation `+` takes precedence (`(5 + 2) == 7`). Thus, the variable `r` is initialized with the value `True`.

Now, we reassign `r`. Let's replace variable names with their corresponding values so that the second to last line becomes `r = True and True and False`.

A sequence of `and` statements is `True` if and only if every element of the sequence is `True`. Since the last element is `False`, the value of `r`, and the result of the puzzle, is `False`.

6.7 Arithmetic Expressions

```
# Elo 1500

r = 3 + 5 - 2
print(type(r))

# this is a comment: / stands for division
# / returns a float value, e.g. 1.523, 5.0,...
r = 4 / 2
print(r)
```

```
# * stands for multiplication
r = 3 * 7
print(type(r))
```

What's the output of this code snippet?
Correct: +10 Elo points / Wrong: -10 Elo points

6.8. INTEGER DIVISION AND MODULO

The puzzle has three major steps.

First, we print the type of the arithmetic expression `3 + 5 - 2` which is an integer i.e. `int`.

Second, we perform the operation *"4 divided by 2"*. The result of any division is a float value because, even if you divide two integers, the result cannot always be represented as an integer (for example `3 / 2 = 1.5`). Considering the correct type here is the biggest challenge of the code puzzle.

Third, we print the type of the resulting value after multiplying two integers `3` and `7`. Multiplying two integers always results in an integer. Hence, the return type of integer multiplication is an `int` too.

6.8 Integer Division and Modulo

```
# Elo 1519

days_count = 219
days_per_week = 7

weeks = days_count // days_per_week
print(weeks)

days = days_count % days_per_week
print(days)
```

What's the output of this code snippet?
Correct: +10 Elo points / Wrong: -10 Elo points

In the code puzzle, we convert a certain number of days into weeks by performing integer division with the `//` operator. The remainder is simply ignored. There are 31 such full weeks.

What is the remainder – how many days are left? The expression `31 * 7 = 217` shows that there are two days left in addition to the `31` full weeks. Hence, the second output of the puzzle (resulting from modulo computation) is `2`. So, the overall output is:

```
31
2
```

6.9 Building Strings

```
# Elo 1472

ha = 'ha'
ho = 'ho'

laughter = 3 * (ha + ho) + '!'

print(laughter)
```

What's the output of this code snippet?
Correct: +10 Elo points / Wrong: -10 Elo points

Here, we have two strings `'ha'` and `'ho'`.

An interesting Python feature is the ability to perform arithmetic operations on strings. The meaning of the + operator on strings is simply *string concatenation*. This means that you glue together the two strings, resulting in the temporary string `haho`.

Then, we multiply this string by **3**. This repeatedly concatenates the temporary string three times. After concatenating `!` to the end, the final result is `hahohahohaho!`.

6.10 The `len()` Function

```
# Elo 1332

my_str = 'cat'
length = len(my_str)

print(length)
```

What's the output of this code snippet?
Correct: +10 Elo points / Wrong: -10 Elo points

6.11. STRING INDICES 79

This puzzle returns the length of the string `'cat'`. The length is the number of characters in a string—which is 3 in this case.

6.11 String Indices

```
# Elo 1571

my_str = 'superman'

print(my_str[0])
print(my_str[1])
print(my_str[len(my_str) - 1])
```

What's the output of this code snippet?
Correct: +10 Elo points / Wrong: -10 Elo points

Here, we use indexing to access three characters at fixed positions in the string `'superman'`.

Note that the first position for any sequence data type starts is `0`, not `1`:

```
s  u  p  e  r  m  a  n
0  1  2  3  4  5  6  7
```

Thus, the final result is:

s
u
n

6.12 The upper() Function

 # Elo 1390

```
text = "Hi, how are you?"
shout = text.upper()

print(shout)
```

What's the output of this code snippet?
Correct: +10 Elo points / Wrong: -10 Elo points

This puzzle converts the string to an uppercase string with each letter capitalized using the string method `upper()`. Hence, the output is: `HI, HOW ARE YOU?`

Note: Python objects have special functions you can just call on them. We call these functions *methods*. The notation to call a method on an object is `object.method()`. In this puzzle, we called the `upper()` method on the string `text` by writing `text.upper()`. As you become more familiar with Python, you will intuitively know which methods can be called on which objects.

6.13 The lower() Function

```
# Elo 1367

text = 'I AM NOT SHOUTING!'
whisper = text.lower()

print(whisper)
```

What's the output of this code snippet?
Correct: +10 Elo points / Wrong: -10 Elo points

In this puzzle, the `lower()` method creates a new lowercase variant of a given string. So, the output is: `i am not shouting!`

6.14 Somebody Is Shouting

```
# Elo 1578

text = 'I AM NOT SHOUTING!'
text.lower()

print(text)
```

What's the output of this code snippet?
Correct: +10 Elo points / Wrong: -10 Elo points

6.15. COUNTING CHARACTERS

This puzzle seems to be similar to the previous puzzle. But it has one important difference: the newly created lowercase variant of the string is not stored anywhere. This highlights the important fact that the `upper()` and `lower()` methods (and other string methods) return a new string rather than modifying an existing string. This is because strings are immutable and so cannot be changed.

We will see other methods which modify the objects they are called on later on in this book.

The output is: I AM NOT SHOUTING!

6.15 Counting Characters

```
# Elo 1543

text = 'Have a nice day.'
space_count = text.count(' ')
total_count = len(text)

print(space_count == total_count)
```

What's the output of this code snippet?
Correct: +10 Elo points / Wrong: -10 Elo points

The puzzle uses the string class's count method to count the number of times the string `'Have a nice day.'` contains the empty space character `' '` (three times).

The length of the string is `16` and it is stored in the variable `total_count`.

Hence, the variables `space_count` and `total_count` have different values and the result of the puzzle is `False`

6.16 String Lengths

```
# Elo 1542

text = 'Have a nice day.'
total_count = len(text)
spaces = total_count * ' '
space_count = len(spaces)

print(space_count == total_count)
```

What's the output of this code snippet?
Correct: +10 Elo points / Wrong: -10 Elo points

Here, we have the same string in the variable `text` as in the previous puzzle.

Both variables `total_count` and `space_count` have the same integer values (`16`). The reason is that the latter is built from the length of the former. It contains `16` times `' '`.

Thus, the result is `True`.

6.17 Finding Characters in Strings

```
# Elo 1501

my_str = 'Donald Duck'
idx = my_str.find('a')

print(idx)
```

What's the output of this code snippet?
Correct: +10 Elo points / Wrong: -10 Elo points

This puzzle uses the string method `find()` to find the index of the first occurrence of `'a'`. In `'Donald Duck'` it is at index 3.

Hence, the result is 3.

6.18 Not Finding Characters in Strings

 # Elo 1334

```
my_str = 'Donald Duck'
idx = my_str.find('y')

print(idx > 0)
```

What's the output of this code snippet?
Correct: +10 Elo points / Wrong: -10 Elo points

6.19. COUNTING LETTERS 87

In this puzzle, we try to find the character `'y'` in the string `'Donald Duck'`.

The letter y does not appear in `my_str`, so `find()` returns `-1`.

Hence, the expression `idx > 0` returns `False`.

6.19 Counting Letters

```
# Elo 1535

letters = 'cheap cars crash'
cs = letters.count('c')
rs = letters.count('r')
ys = letters.count('y')

print(cs - rs > ys)
```

What's the output of this code snippet?
Correct: +10 Elo points / Wrong: -10 Elo points

This puzzle is all about counting characters in the string `'cheap cars crash'`.

The characters are defined as arguments of the `count()` function.

There are three `'c'` characters, two `'r'` characters, and zero `'y'` characters in the string.

Thus, the result is `3 - 2 > 0` which is `True`.

6.20 Min() and Max() of a String

 # Elo 1470

```
my_str = 'python'
print(min(my_str) + max(my_str))
```

What's the output of this code snippet?
Correct: +10 Elo points / Wrong: -10 Elo points

6.21. REVERSED STRINGS

This puzzle delivers one important piece of information: you can use the minimum and maximum function on strings—even though they are not of a numerical type.

A string is a sequence of characters—and characters can be sorted alphabetically (you may have heard the formal name *lexicographical sort*). Naturally, the minimum of a collection of characters is the character that comes first in the alphabet. Similarly, the maximum is the character that comes last in the alphabet.

So, the result is hy.

6.21 Reversed Strings

```
# Elo 1398

my_str = 'python'
print(my_str[::-1])
```

What's the output of this code snippet?
Correct: +10 Elo points / Wrong: -10 Elo points

This is the first puzzle that introduces slice notation on a sequence type (in this case a string).

Generally, slicing selects a subsequence of elements from a sequence.

The notation is [start:stop:step].

The subsequence starts at the element with index **start** and goes until the element with index **end**.

Note that the **start** index is included and the **end** index is excluded from the slice.

Finally, the **step** size defines the index difference between elements. For example, **step = 2** selects every other character. Setting **step = -1** selects elements in reverse order, i.e., from right to left.

The slice in this puzzle does not define the **start** or **stop** indices. Thus it includes all characters (the default behaviour).

Thus, the result is the full original string in reverse: **nohtyp**.

6.22 String Equality

```
# Elo 1410

my_str = 'python'
```

6.22. STRING EQUALITY

```
are_equal = my_str[:] == my_str

print(are_equal)
```

What's the output of this code snippet?
Correct: +10 Elo points / Wrong: -10 Elo points

In this puzzle, we check whether two strings with the same characters are equal using the equality operator `==`.

We use slicing with default values to create a string with the same characters as the original string `'my_str'`.

Thus, both strings are equal and `True` is the output for this puzzle.

6.23 Slicing I

```
# Elo 1431

my_str = 'python'
my_substring = my_str[4:]

print(my_substring)
```

What's the output of this code snippet?
Correct: +10 Elo points / Wrong: -10 Elo points

In this puzzle, we use slicing with start index 4. So, we start the subsequence at the fifth character because indexing starts at 0.

Therefore, the result of this puzzle is `on`.

6.24 Slicing II

```
# Elo 1598

my_str = 'python'
my_substr = my_str[::2]

print(my_substr)
```

What's the output of this code snippet?
Correct: +10 Elo points / Wrong: -10 Elo points

In this puzzle, we use slicing with default values to create a string with the same characters as the original string. But we access every second element by setting (`step = 2`).

Thus, the result is `pto`.

6.25 Slicing III

```
# Elo 1591

my_str = 'AaBbCcDdEeFf'
big = my_str[::2]
small = my_str[1::2]

print(big + '-' + small)
```

What's the output of this code snippet?
Correct: +10 Elo points / Wrong: -10 Elo points

6.26. SLICING IV

In this puzzle, we first define a mini alphabet.

Then we slice every second character on the second and third lines.

In the first case, (`big`), we start with the first sequence element. In the second case ,(`small`), we start with the second sequence element.

Thus, the first slice returns all capitalized letters and the second slice returns all lowercase letters:

`ABCDEF-abcdef`

6.26 Slicing IV

```
# Elo 1588

chars_1 = 'Rzotbo'
chars_2 = 'tigno'

mystery = chars_1[::2] + chars_2[1::2]

print(mystery)
```

What's the output of this code snippet?
Correct: +10 Elo points / Wrong: -10 Elo points

This puzzle concatenates the results of two slice operations on two strings and stores it in the variable `mystery`.

The first slice operation takes every second value and returns `'Rob'`.

The second takes every second value starting from the second element and returns `'in'`.

When concatenated together, the final result is `Robin`.

6.27 Slicing V

```
# Elo 1395

my_str = 'Batman'
other_str = my_str[0:len(my_str)]

print(other_str)
```

What's the output of this code snippet?
Correct: +10 Elo points / Wrong: -10 Elo points

The main challenge of this puzzle is determining the result of the slicing operation in the second line.

We start at the first sequence element and slice until we reach the index `len(my_str)` (= 6). Note that slicing never includes the end index, so the last index included is 5.

Thus, it consists of the original characters `Batman`.

6.28 Memory Addresses and Slicing

```
# Elo 1501

my_str = 'Aquaman'
id_1 = id(my_str)

my_str = my_str[4:]
id_2 = id(my_str)

print(id_1 == id_2)
```

What's the output of this code snippet?
Correct: +10 Elo points / Wrong: -10 Elo points

This puzzle takes the id of two strings and compares them.

The function `id()` returns a unique identifier (integer value) for all objects in memory.

The real question is whether `my_str` referred to two different memory locations?

Let me emphasize that the slice operation creates a new string and does not modify an existing string. This is because strings are immutable—they cannot be changed. Each time you perform a slice operation or concatenate two strings, you create a new object in memory.

Thus, this puzzle's output is `False`.

6.29 Accessing List Items I

```
# Elo 1567

my_list = [
    'apple',
    'banana',
    'orange',
]

item = my_list[len(my_list)-2]
print(item)
```

6.29. ACCESSING LIST ITEMS I

What's the output of this code snippet?
Correct: +10 Elo points / Wrong: -10 Elo points

In this puzzle, we create a list of three strings.

Then, we use indexing to select elements in the list. The index is `len(my_list) - 2 = 3 - 2 = 1`.

So, the item to be printed is `banana`.

6.30 Accessing List Items II

```
# Elo 1340

my_list = [
    'apple',
    'orange',
    'banana',
]

item = my_list[1]

print(item)
```

What's the output of this code snippet?
Correct: +10 Elo points / Wrong: -10 Elo points

With the help of Python's simple indexing scheme, we return the second element (index equal to one).

Thus, the result is `orange`.

6.31 List as Stack

```
# Elo 1499

my_list = [
    'apple',
    'banana',
    'orange',
]

item = my_list.pop()

print(item)
```

What's the output of this code snippet?
Correct: +10 Elo points / Wrong: -10 Elo points

Similar to the last puzzle, the list contains three string elements.

We use the `pop()` method to remove the last element from the list (`'orange'`). This is returned and assigned to the variable `item`.

Note that the `pop()` method can be used to easily implement a stack data structure in Python.

This puzzle's output is `orange`.

6.32 More String Operations

```
# Elo 1461

phone = 'smartphone'
x = phone.startswith('smart')
y = phone.endswith('phone')

print(x and y)
```

What's the output of this code snippet?
Correct: +10 Elo points / Wrong: -10 Elo points

6.33. CHECKING FOR SUBSTRINGS

This puzzle checks two things: does the string `'smartphone'`

1. start with the prefix `'smart'`, and
2. end with the suffix `'phone'`?

This is the case, so the result is `True`.

6.33 Checking for Substrings

```
# Elo 1133

phone = 'smartphone'
x = 'xyz' in phone

print(not x)
```

What's the output of this code snippet?
Correct: +10 Elo points / Wrong: -10 Elo points

Now, we use the same string as before to check whether a certain substring exists in this string.

Note that a string is a sequence so you can check whether a subsequence exists within it.

The string `'smartphone'` does not contain the subsequence `'xyz'`.

Hence, the result is `True`, i.e., `not False`.

6.34 Stripping String Boundaries

```
# Elo 1455

sentence = ' Python is cool! '
sentence = sentence.strip()
x = sentence.endswith(' ')

print(x)
```

What's the output of this code snippet?
Correct: +10 Elo points / Wrong: -10 Elo points

Let's consider the string `sentence` in the puzzle. It has leading and trailing whitespaces.

The `strip()` method is a very useful tool for text processing tasks: it removes any leading and trailing whitespaces.

So, the result is `False`.

6.35 Strings: Stripping vs. Replacement

```
# Elo 1555

sentence = '  Python is cool!  '
str_1 = sentence.strip()
str_2 = sentence.replace(' ', '')

print(str_1 == str_2)
```

What's the output of this code snippet?
Correct: +10 Elo points / Wrong: -10 Elo points

This puzzle is similar to the last one but with one difference: the second string does not strip leading and trailing whitespaces. Instead, it replaces all occurrences of the whitespace character ' ' with the empty string. This is the same as removing all whitespace in the sentence.

While `str_1` still has some whitespaces left (in between each word), `str_2` does not.

So, the result of the final print statement is `False`.

6.36 Gluing Strings Together

```
# Elo 1419

shopping_list = [
    'bread',
    'milk',
    'cheese',
]

string = ','.join(shopping_list)

print(string)
```

What's the output of this code snippet?
Correct: +10 Elo points / Wrong: -10 Elo points

The shopping list contains three items: bread, milk, and cheese.

The `join()` method is a well-known string method. It combines a collection elements using the separator string on which the method was called. The separator is used to glue together the individual list elements.

So, it returns the final string `break,milk,cheese`.

Note there is no space between each item because the separator string did not contain a space.

6.37 The Copy Operation

```
# Elo 1489

my_list = [
    'Bob',
    'Alice',
    'Donald',
    'Goofy',
]

your_list = my_list.copy()

print(id(your_list) == id(my_list))
```

What's the output of this code snippet?

CHAPTER 6. PUZZLES: SCHOLAR TO INTERMEDIATE

Correct: +10 Elo points / Wrong: -10 Elo points

6.38. GROWING LIST CONTENTS I 109

This puzzle first copies the given list. Then it checks whether the copy and the original list refer to the same element in memory. This is not the case: the new list represents a different object.

So, the result of comparing the two lists is `False`.

6.38 Growing List Contents I

```
# Elo 1480

my_list = []

my_list.append('Tomato')
my_list = my_list + ['Pizza']

print(my_list)
```

What's the output of this code snippet?
Correct: +10 Elo points / Wrong: -10 Elo points

First, we create an empty list and append the string `'Tomato'`.

Second, we concatenate two lists together with the + operator.

Thus, the result is a new list `['Tomato', 'Pizza']`.

6.39 Growing List Contents II

```
# Elo 1427

odd = [1, 3, 5, 7]
even = [0, 2, 4, 6]

odd.extend(even)

print(len(odd))
```

What's the output of this code snippet?
Correct: +10 Elo points / Wrong: -10 Elo points

6.39. GROWING LIST CONTENTS II

Surprisingly, many students don't know the `extend()` method despite being perfectly aware of the `append()` method.

If you want to add a single element to a list, the `append()` method is all you need.

What if you want to add multiple elements? Beginner coders often use one of the following options:

1. they create a for loop and append a single element multiple times, or
2. they use the list concatenation operator '+' e.g. [3, 2] + [1, 2] => [3, 2, 1, 2])

The problem with the former is that it's inefficient to modify a list n times to append n elements.

The problem with the latter is that it creates a completely new list which is both time and space inefficient—especially for large lists.

The solution is simple: use the `extend()` method. It appends multiple elements to a list in a single operation.

Although it is semantically doing the same thing as calling `append()` multiple times, `extend()` is much more efficient. This is because it's implemented in low-level C code and is highly optimized towards this specific objective. Always use `extend()` if you want to append multiple elements to a list!

The result of this puzzle is the list [1, 3, 5, 7, 0, 2, 4, 6] so the length is 8.

6.40 List Operations I

 # Elo 1381

```
my_list = []
my_list.append(1)
my_list.append(2)
my_list.pop()

print(len(my_list))
```

What's the output of this code snippet?
Correct: +10 Elo points / Wrong: -10 Elo points

6.41. LIST OPERATIONS II 113

First, we create an empty list and add some values (1 and 2) to it.

Second, we remove the last element (2) from the list. So, the list has only one element left.

Thus, the result is 1.

6.41 List Operations II

```
# Elo 1441

my_list = [4, 5, 6]
index = 0
my_list.insert(index, 3)

print(my_list[1])
```

What's the output of this code snippet?
Correct: +10 Elo points / Wrong: -10 Elo points

This puzzle inserts the element 3 at position 0 in the list.

The resulting list looks like this: [3, 4, 5, 6].

The second element is printed to the shell which is 4.

6.42 List Operations III

```
# Elo 1485

my_list = [1, 2, 3, 4]
value = 2
index = 2
my_list.remove(value)

print(my_list[index])
```

What's the output of this code snippet?
Correct: +10 Elo points / Wrong: -10 Elo points

6.43. LIST OPERATIONS IV 115

In this puzzle, we remove the first occurrence of the element `'2'` from `my_list`. The result is [1, 3, 4].

We now print the third element and the result is 4.

6.43 List Operations IV

```
# Elo 1469

my_list = [1, 2, 3, 3, 2, 3]
index = my_list.index(3)

print(index)
```

What's the output of this code snippet?
Correct: +10 Elo points / Wrong: -10 Elo points

The `index(x)` method returns the index of the first occurrence of `x` in the sequence on which it is called.

In this case, we are looking for the value `x = 3`. There are three such occurrences but only the first one is returned to the function: index 2.

Therefore, the result is 2.

6.44 List Operations V

 # Elo 1399

```
my_list = [1, 2, 3, 0, 2, 3]
count = my_list.count(3)

print(count)
```

What's the output of this code snippet?
Correct: +10 Elo points / Wrong: -10 Elo points

After creating the list, we call the `count(x)` method to count the number of occurrences of `x = 3` in the list.

There are two such occurrences, so the result is 2.

6.45 List Operations VI

 # Elo 1311

```
my_list = ['car', 'bike', 'boat']
my_list.clear()

print(len(my_list))
```

What's the output of this code snippet?
Correct: +10 Elo points / Wrong: -10 Elo points

Here, we create a new list with three elements and we `clear()` the list immediately after. This removes all elements from the list so that the list is empty.

The resulting length is, therefore, 0.

6.46 List Operations VII

 # Elo 1501

```
my_list = [4, 7, 3, 9, 1]
my_list.sort()

print(my_list)
```

What's the output of this code snippet?
Correct: +10 Elo points / Wrong: -10 Elo points

CHAPTER 6. PUZZLES: SCHOLAR TO INTERMEDIATE

The puzzle is simple but introduces a profound piece of knowledge for your Python education: *sorting lists*. Just call the `sort()` method on any list and it returns the list in ascending order.

Some Finxters are trapped by this puzzle because they think the `sort()` method returns a new list with sorted values. This is not the case, the original list is modified. This is because lists are mutable objects, i.e., they can be modified.

Thus, the result is [1, 3, 4, 7, 9].

6.47 List Operations VIII

```
# Elo 1333

my_list = [10, 9, 8, 7]
my_list.reverse()

print(my_list)
```

What's the output of this code snippet?
Correct: +10 Elo points / Wrong: -10 Elo points

6.48. LIST OPERATIONS IX 119

This puzzle reverses the order of the list elements.

As with sorting, the list itself is changed (Python does not create a new list of reversed elements).

Thus, the output is [7, 8, 9, 10].

6.48 List Operations IX

```
# Elo 1498

my_list = [False, False, True]
x = any(my_list)

print(x)
```

What's the output of this code snippet?
Correct: +10 Elo points / Wrong: -10 Elo points

This puzzle tests your intuitive understanding of the function any().

Maybe you've never used it in your code projects – but you can figure out what it does when applied to a Boolean collection, right?

It checks whether "any" of the elements are True.

In this case, the third list element is True, so the result is True.

6.49 List Operations X

```
# Elo 1532

bool_val = all([
    1 == 1,
    7 // 2 == 2 + 1,
    2 == 6 % 4,
])

print(bool_val)
```

What's the output of this code snippet?
Correct: +10 Elo points / Wrong: -10 Elo points

This puzzle goes one step further. You need to figure out multiple logical expressions before testing whether `all()` of them are `True`.

The first expression `1==1` is obviously `True`. The second expression is also `True` because 7 // 2 = 3 = 2 + 1. Finally, the third expression is `True` as *six modulo four is 2*.

Thus, the `all()` function returns `True`.

6.50 Lists and the Range Function I

```
# Elo 1300

len_of_list = len(list(range(10)))
print(len_of_list)
```

What's the output of this code snippet?
Correct: +10 Elo points / Wrong: -10 Elo points

In this puzzle, we first create a new list with sequence values from 0 to 9 (inclusive).

It is very common for beginners to miss this. For the vast majority of Python functions, the stop value is excluded – it's not part of the returned sequence. This is also `True` for advanced Python libraries for data science and machine learning like NumPy and TensorFlow. So learn it now and learn it well!

As there are ten elements in the list, the result is the integer value 10.

6.51 Lists and the Range Function II

```
# Elo 1440

l = list(range(5, 15, 5))
print(l)
```

What's the output of this code snippet?
Correct: +10 Elo points / Wrong: -10 Elo points

Similar to the last puzzle, this one tests your understanding of the range function.

The function `range(start, stop, step)` returns a sequence of values starting at index `start` (inclusive), ending at index `stop` (exclusive), and including every `step`-th value.

So, the final result is the list `[5, 10]`.

6.52 Lists and the Range Function III

```
# Elo 1456

l = list(range(10, 1, -1))
print(l)
```

What's the output of this code snippet?
Correct: +10 Elo points / Wrong: −10 Elo points

This time, the range function has a negative step size. This means that the resulting sequence has descending values.

We start at position 10(inclusive) and end at position 1 (exclusive).

Thus, the result is [10, 9, 8, 7, 6, 5, 4, 3, 2].

6.53 Python's Multiple Assignment I

```
# Elo 1302

a = 'world!'
b = 'hello '

b, a = a, b

print(a + b)
```

What's the output of this code snippet?
Correct: +10 Elo points / Wrong: -10 Elo points

The puzzle creates two string variables and swaps them using concise multiple assignment notation:

```
b, a = a, b
```

The Python interpreter performs two steps:

1. evaluate the right-hand side of the equation, then
2. assign the results to the variables on the left-hand side.

In the example, we swap the values of a and b.

Thus, the result is the concatenated string hello world!

6.54 Slice Assignments

```
# Elo 1507

my_list = [1, 1, 1, 1]
my_list[1::2] = [2, 3]

print(my_list)
```

What's the output of this code snippet?
Correct: +10 Elo points / Wrong: -10 Elo points

CHAPTER 6. PUZZLES: SCHOLAR TO INTERMEDIATE

The puzzle trains your understanding of an interesting Python feature: *slice assignments* to replace subsequences.

First, we create the list `'my_list'` with four integer values.

Second, we select the elements to be replaced using slice notation `[start:stop:step]` on the left-hand side of the equation.

Starting with the second list element (index 1), we take every other element (step size 2). This means we will replace the second and fourth elements.

Third, we define the elements that to replace the selected elements (2 and 3).

The result of the puzzle is, therefore, [1, 2, 1, 3].

6.55 Strings and Lists II

```
# Elo 1467

my_list = ['1, 2, 3', '4, 5']
print(len(my_list))
```

What's the output of this code snippet?
Correct: +10 Elo points / Wrong: -10 Elo points

6.56. STRING COMPARISONS

The challenge in this puzzle is to read code thoroughly.

Although it may look like there are five elements in the list, there are only two. The first element is the string `'1, 2, 3'` and the second element is the string `'4, 5'`.

Therefore, the length of the list is 2.

6.56 String Comparisons

```
# Elo 1419

word = 'radar'
p = word == word[::-1]

print(p)
```

What's the output of this code snippet?
Correct: +10 Elo points / Wrong: -10 Elo points

A palindrome is a word that reads the same forward and backward. In this puzzle, we check to see if `'radar'` is a palindrome.

First, we create a string `'radar'` and store the Boolean result of (`word == word[::-1]`).

The right-hand side of the equation reverses the characters in the string.

As it turns out, `'radar'` reads the same forward and backwards and so it's a palindrome.

Thus, the result is `True`.

6.57 From Booleans to Strings

```
# Elo 1549

value_0 = int(True)
value_1 = int(False)
string = str(value_0) + str(value_1)

print(string)
```

What's the output of this code snippet?
Correct: +10 Elo points / Wrong: -10 Elo points

6.58. BOOLEAN TRICKERY I

This workout tests your understanding of three Python data types: Boolean, integer and string.

Boolean values are internally represented as integers: 0 being `False` and 1 being `True`. When converting a Boolean to an integer, use this mapping.

Before we add them together, we convert them to strings.

Thus, the + operator performs concatenation rather than integer addition.

The result is 10.

Note that when an operator performs different actions for different data types, we say this operator is *overloaded*.

6.58 Boolean Trickery I

```
# Elo 1309

print(1000 * False)
```

What's the output of this code snippet?
Correct: +10 Elo points / Wrong: -10 Elo points

As you already know, the value `False` is represented as an integer 0 in Python.

If you multiply 0 with anything, you get 0.

So, the result is 0.

6.59 Boolean Trickery II

```
# Elo 1324

print((3 == 4) == 0)
```

What's the output of this code snippet?
Correct: +10 Elo points / Wrong: -10 Elo points

6.60. BOOLEAN TRICKERY III 131

When using operators, binary or otherwise, the order of operation matters.

You can enforce a certain order of operations using bracket notation.

In the puzzle, we first evaluate the expression (`3 == 4`) which is `False`.

Next, we compare `False` with `0`.

As Python represents Boolean values with integers (`False` by `0`) the puzzle's result is `True`.

6.60 Boolean Trickery III

```
# Elo 1388

print(bool([]))
```

What's the output of this code snippet?
Correct: +10 Elo points / Wrong: -10 Elo points

Python allows you to convert any object to a Boolean value.

This is useful for concise `if` and `while` loop conditions – you'll see this a lot in practice.

You already know that an integer value 0 is converted to the Boolean value of `False`. But which other objects are converted to `False`?

By default, *every object* is converted to `True` with a few exceptions:

- empty sequences,
- 0,
- 0.0,
- empty sets or dictionaries `{}`,
- certain *empty objects* e.g. empty lists

Thus, the result is `False`.

6.61 Looping over Ranges

```
# Elo 1422

n = 0
```

6.61. LOOPING OVER RANGES

```
for i in range(0, 6, 3):
    n += i

print(n)
```

What's the output of this code snippet?
Correct: +10 Elo points / Wrong: -10 Elo points

The loop variable i takes on two values: i = 0 and i = 3.

It does not take on i = 6 because the stop value is always excluded in range sequences `range(0, 6, 3)`.

Therefore, the sum variable n stores the integer 0 + 3 = 3 which is the result of the puzzle.

6.62 Reversed Loops

```
# Elo 1453

str_ = ''

for c in reversed('nohtyp'):
    str_ += c

print(str_)
```

What's the output of this code snippet?
Correct: +10 Elo points / Wrong: -10 Elo points

6.63. BOOLEAN TRICKERY IV 135

The built-in function `reversed(x)` creates an iterator - an object you can loop over. It visits the elements in the sequence `x` in reverse order.

In our case, x = 'nohtyp'.

The result is this sequence of characters reversed i.e. `python`.

6.63 Boolean Trickery IV

```
# Elo 1347

s = sum([
    True,
    False,
    True,
    True,
])

print(s)
```

What's the output of this code snippet?
Correct: +10 Elo points / Wrong: -10 Elo points

Have you studied the previous explanations thoroughly? Then you should have had no problem with this puzzle!

The Boolean value `True` is represented by `1` and the Boolean value `False` is represented by `0`.

So, when summing over the list of Boolean values, the result is 1 + 0 + 1 + 1 = 3

6.64 Lists and Memory Addresses

```
# Elo 1391

my_list = []
id_1 = id(my_list)

my_list = my_list + [1]
id_2 = id(my_list)

print(id_1 == id_2)
```

What's the output of this code snippet?
Correct: +10 Elo points / Wrong: -10 Elo points

6.65. LIST OBJECTS   137

In the first line we create a new list object and assign it to the variable `my_list`.

Then we use the built-in function `id(x)` to get the memory address of it.

When we concatenate `my_list` with `[1]` and assign it to `my_list`, a new list object is created. So, the reference stored in `my_list` changes.

This is why `id_1` is different from `id_2` and the comparison returns `False`.

6.65 List Objects

```
# Elo 1399

my_list = []
id_1 = id(my_list)

my_list.append(1)
id_2 = id(my_list)

print(id_1 == id_2)
```

What's the output of this code snippet?
Correct: +10 Elo points / Wrong: -10 Elo points

The code in this puzzle is similar to the code in the previous one with an important difference: instead of concatenating the lists, we append a new value using `list.append(x)`.

This does not create a new object because we modify the old list rather than creating a new one from scratch.

Therefore, we have the same memory address both before and after appending the value.

Thus, the result is `True`.

6.66 Boolean Tricks

```
# Elo 1486

b = all([
    bool('0'),
    bool('?'),
    bool('-'),
    bool('e'),
])

print(b)
```

What's the output of this code snippet?
Correct: +10 Elo points / Wrong: -10 Elo points

Python lets you convert a string to a Boolean.

The rule is simple: any string longer than zero characters is `True`.

Only the empty string `''` is `False`.

In fact, you can specify a Boolean value for any object in Python by defining its `__bool__(self)` method in a custom class definition.

Python's built-in `all(x)` function checks if all Boolean values in the container are `True`.

Since there is no empty string in the list, the result is `True`.

6.67 Complex Numbers

```
# Elo 1575

a = complex(2, 4)
b = complex(1, -3)

print(a + b)
```

What's the output of this code snippet?
Correct: +10 Elo points / Wrong: -10 Elo points

From time to time, you'll need to use complex numbers for graphical applications, data analysis or simulations.

Simply use the built-in `Complex` class to represent complex numbers. The constructor `Complex` accepts two values. The first is the real part and the second is the (optional) imaginary part. For example, `complex(1)` yields `(1 + 0j)`.

The sum of two complex numbers is the sum of their real values plus the sum of their imaginary values.

In this puzzle, the real part is `2 + 1 = 3` and the imaginary-part is `4 + (-3) = 1`.

The result, therefore, is `(3+1j)`.

6.68 Tuples

```
# Elo 1462

x = 'a', 'b', 'c'
y = 3,

print(type(x) == type(y))
```

What's the output of this code snippet?
Correct: +10 Elo points / Wrong: -10 Elo points

The objects defined in this puzzle are tuples. It's a bit tricky because the puzzle uses tuple notation without parentheses.

You can define a tuple in two ways:

1. `t1 = (1, 2)`, or
2. `t2 = 1, 2`.

Both are equivalent.

In the puzzle, the values of x and y are tuples.

So the result of the type comparison is `True`.

6.69 Multiple Assignments

```
# Elo 1478

x, y, z = 'cat'

print(y)
```

What's the output of this code snippet?
Correct: +10 Elo points / Wrong: -10 Elo points

The puzzle demonstrates a very important feature in Python that you'll see a lot in the real world.

We assign the string `'cat'` to three different variables in one line:

- the value of x is `'c'`,
- the value of y is `'a'`,
- the value of z is `'t'`.

So printing y returns a.

6.70 Boolean Integer Conversion

```
# Elo 1543

my_bools = []

for n in range(-1, -10, -1):
    my_bools.append(bool(n))

result = all(my_bools)

print(result)
```

What's the output of this code snippet?
Correct: +10 Elo points / Wrong: -10 Elo points

6.71. THE ANY() FUNCTION

Python automatically converts integers to Booleans if Boolean values are expected.

The rule is simple: `0` is `False` and all other integers are `True`.

Converting Boolean values back to integers is also simple: `True` is the integer `1` and `False` is the integer value `0`.

In the puzzle, we iterate over the values -1, -2, -3, ... -9—using the `range()` function with negative step size—and convert them to Boolean values.

As none of the values are 0, Python converts them all to `True`.

Using the built-in `all(x)` function, we check if all values in the list are `True`. This is the case, so the result is `True`.

6.71 The any() Function

```
# Elo 1593

b = any([
    bool(None),
    bool(0),
    bool(dict()),
])
```

```
print(b)
```

What's the output of this code snippet?
Correct: +10 Elo points / Wrong: -10 Elo points

Python's built-in function `any(container)` checks if `container` contains any value that evaluates to `True`.

In the previous puzzle, you learned that the 0 is converted to `False`. Similarly, `None` also evaluates to `False`.

To convert a container (list, dictionary, set,...) to a Boolean, follow this rule:

A container `c` is `True` if and only if:

1. it exists, and

2. `len(c) > 0`

Thus, the Boolean value of an empty dictionary is `False`.

Therefore, the list contains three `False` values.

So, `any(...)` returns `False`.

6.72 The `sum()` Function

```
# Elo 1482

my_list = [1, 1, 0]
s = 3

if my_list:
    s = sum(my_list)
```

```
print(s)
```

What's the output of this code snippet?
Correct: +10 Elo points / Wrong: -10 Elo points

The puzzle tests your understanding of two concepts you've already seen:

- Boolean values of containers and
- Summing over Boolean values.

In Python, it's common to use Boolean auto conversion statements such as `if my_list:`.

In plain English, read it as: "If `my_list` is not equal to `None` and has at least one element, do the following."

Since `my_list` contains three elements, the code inside the branch is executed and `s` is set to the sum of all elements in the list: 1 + 1 + 0 = 2.

6.73 Accessing Complex Numbers

```
# Elo 1571

a = complex(2, 5)
b = complex(a.imag, a.real)

print(b)
```

What's the output of this code snippet?
Correct: +10 Elo points / Wrong: -10 Elo points

6.74. TUPLE CONFUSION

You can access the real-part of a complex number with its `.real` attribute and the imaginary part with the `.imag` attribute.

We use those two values to create a new complex number that has swapped the real and imaginary parts of `a`.

So, `b` is `(5+2j)`.

Note: attributes and methods look similar when applied to objects. Remember that you do not place () after attributes but you do for methods.

6.74 Tuple Confusion

```
# Elo 1479

p1 = (1, -1)
p2 = (2, 5)
p3 = (p1[0] + p2[0], p1[1] + p2[1])

print(p3)
```

What's the output of this code snippet?
Correct: +10 Elo points / Wrong: -10 Elo points

This puzzle is all about tuples.

The values of a tuple can be retrieved using brackets and an index value.

Like all other Python indexing, we use index 0 to access the first element, index 1 to access the second element and so on.

In this puzzle, we create a new tuple by adding the values of p1 and p2.

So, the value of p3 is: (1 + 2, -1 + 5) = (3, 4).

6.75 Understanding While ... Else (1/3)

```
# Elo 1561

index = 5
s = 'g'

while index > 3:
    index -= 1
    s += 'o'
else:
    s += 'd'

print(s)
```

What's the output of this code snippet?
Correct: +10 Elo points / Wrong: -10 Elo points

Python has a special loop statement called the *while-else loop*.

The body of the `while` part is repeated until the condition is not met anymore.

The `else` statement only executes if the while loop finishes because its condition has become `False`.

If Python exits the `while` loop *prematurely* via a `break` statement, the `else` part is not executed.

In this puzzle, the while loop is executed twice with `index = 5` and `index = 4`). This appends `'oo'` to the initial string `'g'` in the variable `s`.

In the next step, the condition of the while loop becomes `False` and the else part executes.

In the else branch, Python adds `'d'` to the variable `s`.

So, the final result is good.

6.76 Understanding While ... Else (2/3)

```
# Elo 1578

index = 5
string = 'g'
```

6.76. UNDERSTANDING WHILE ... ELSE (2/3)

```
while index > 3:
    index -= 1
    string += 'o'
    break
else:
    string += 'd'

print(string)
```

What's the output of this code snippet?
Correct: +10 Elo points / Wrong: -10 Elo points

This puzzle is similar to the previous puzzle.

Initially, `string` only contains the character `'g'`.

Then, the while loop is executed and adds the character `'o'` to the variable `string`.

However, the loop ends prematurely because of the `break` statement.

Thus, the `else` branch is not executed and the result is go.

6.77 Understanding While ... Else (3/3)

```
# Elo 1571

index = 5
string = 'g'

while index > 3:
    index -= 1
    if index == 3:
        continue
    string += 'o'

else:
    string += 'd'
```

```
print(string)
```

What's the output of this code snippet?
Correct: +10 Elo points / Wrong: -10 Elo points

Again, the puzzle shows a similar code snippet as in the previous two puzzles. The only difference is that when `index == 3`, the execution goes back to the beginning of the while-loop because of the `continue` statement.

The loop body executes twice for `index = 5` and `index = 4` but only the first round adds the character `'o'` to `string`.

In the second round, the index is set to `3`. Thus, Python enters the `if` branch that contains the `continue` statement.

After this, the while condition is evaluated again. Since the value of `index` is 3, the while condition evaluates to `False`.

So, Python executes the else branch. The last step adds the character `'d'` to `string` and the final output is god.

6.78 Basic Arithmetic

```
# Elo 1419

def magic(x, y):
    return x ** y + 1

print(magic(2, 3))
```

What's the output of this code snippet?

6.78. BASIC ARITHMETIC

Correct: +10 Elo points / Wrong: -10 Elo points

We define a function with two arguments: x and y.

The function computes x to the power of y - x ** y - and adds one.

We call the function with x = 2 and y = 3 and get (2 * 2 * 2) + 1 = 9

6.79 Dictionary

```
# Elo 1531

dict_ = {
    1: 'one',
    2: 'two',
    3: 'three',
}

def to_str(number):
    if number in dict_:
        return dict_[number]
    else:
        return '?'

s1 = to_str(2)
s2 = to_str(7)

print(s1 + s2)
```

6.79. DICTIONARY

What's the output of this code snippet?
Correct: +10 Elo points / Wrong: -10 Elo points

The puzzle shows how to create and access the dictionary data structure in Python.

First, we create the dictionary `dict_`.

Then we create the function `to_str`. It takes a single argument `number` and checks if it is present among the keys of `dict_`. If it is present, it returns its corresponding value. Otherwise, it returns the string `'?'`.

After defining the function, we use it to initialize two variables `s1` and `s2`.

For `s1`, the value returned by `to_str(2)` is `'two'` because 2 is one of the keys of `dict_`.

For `s2`, the value returned by `to_str(7)` is `'?'` because 7 is not a key of `dict_`.

By printing the concatenation of the two strings, we get `'two?'`.

6.80 Dictionary of Dictionaries

```
# Elo 1501

sales = {
    100: {'item': 'apple', 'price': .95},
    101: {'item': 'banana', 'price': .55},
    102: {'item': 'orange', 'price': .75},
}
```

6.80. DICTIONARY OF DICTIONARIES

```
value = sales[102].get('price')

print(value)
```

What's the output of this code snippet?
Correct: +10 Elo points / Wrong: -10 Elo points

The variable `sales` is initialized as a dictionary of dictionaries. Each value of `sales` represents the sold item's name and price.

First, we access the full dictionary of item 102 using bracket notation `sales[102]`.

To get the price, we call the `get()` method and pass the string `'price'`.

Thus the value stored in `value` is 0.75.

Note that calling the `get()` method is an alternative way to access a value. Writing `sales[102].get('price')` is the same as writing `sales[102]['price']`.

An advantage of using `get()` is that it returns `None` if the key is not present in the dictionary.

In contrast, if you use square brackets `[]` and try to access key-value pairs that do not exist, Python raises a `KeyError` which you must handle appropriately to avoid a program crash.

6.81 Reverse Dictionary Index

```
# Elo 1533

roman = {
    1: 'I', 2: 'II', 3: 'III', 4: 'IV', 5: 'V',
    6: 'VI', 7: 'VII', 8: 'VIII', 9: 'IX', 10: 'X'
```

6.81. REVERSE DICTIONARY INDEX

```
}

arab = {}

for key, value in roman.items():
    arab[value] = key

print(arab['VII'])
```

What's the output of this code snippet?
Correct: +10 Elo points / Wrong: -10 Elo points

The variable `roman` is initialized as a dictionary. Its keys are the Arabic numerals from 1-10 and the values are their corresponding roman numeral strings.

To store the reverse mapping from roman numeral strings to Arabic numbers, we first initialize an empty dictionary `arab`.

Then we iterate over the (arab, roman) pairs in `roman` using the `items()` method.

For each pair, we set the roman string as the key `arab[value]` and set the Arabic numeral as its value = `key`.

Hence, when printing `arab['VII']`, Python outputs the Arabic numeral 7.

6.82 Default Arguments

```
# Elo 1531

def func(a, b, c = 5):
    return a + b + c

r1 = func(1, 0)
r2 = func(1, 1, 2)

print(r1 < r2)
```

What's the output of this code snippet?

6.82. DEFAULT ARGUMENTS

Correct: +10 Elo points / Wrong: -10 Elo points

This puzzle shows you how to overload your own functions. Now you can write one function that takes a different number of arguments.

We define the function `func` with three arguments. The first two arguments are required—you have to specify them every time you call the function.

However, the third argument `c` is optional and has a default value of 5. This means that if you call `func` with two arguments, `c` is assumed to be 5.

Hence, variable `r1` holds the value 6 (1 + 0 + 5) while variable `r2` holds the value 4 (1 + 1 + 2).

In the latter case, the value of `c` is specified as 2—overwriting the default value 5.

Therefore, the print statement at the end evaluates to 6 < 4 = `False`.

— 7 —

Python Puzzles: From *Intermediate* to *Professional* Level

Have you tracked your Elo rating throughout the book? You should already have seen a significant improvement in your Elo rating by now. The puzzles that follow are even harder and range from Elo 1600 to Elo 1900. If you can solve these correctly, you can consider yourself an above-average coder and will soon be at a professional level.

7.1 Building Strings II

```
# Elo 1600

chars = 'dog!'
```

```
char_1 = chars[-2]
char_2 = chars[chars.find('o')]
char_3 = chars[-1]

print(char_1 + char_2 + char_3)
```

What's the output of this code snippet?
Correct: +10 Elo points / Wrong: -10 Elo points

7.2. STRING: SLICING AND INDEXING

The puzzle uses negative indexing on the string `'dog!'`.

Negative indexing is a way of accessing the string from right-to-left instead of from left-to-right. For example, the index `-1` accesses the last character of the string. The index `-2` accesses the second last character and so on. This way, you can decide on the more convenient way of accessing the specific characters you want.

In the puzzle, we start with the second last character `'g'`. Then, we access the character at the `chars.find('o')` = 1 position which is `'o'`. Finally, we access the last character `'!'`.

The print statement prints the concatenated characters to the shell which is the string `go!`.

7.2 String: Slicing and Indexing

```
# Elo 1611

chars = 'bretsamaty'
word = chars[1:7][::-1]

print(word)
```

What's the output of this code snippet?
Correct: +10 Elo points / Wrong: -10 Elo points

In contrast to the previous slicing puzzles, this puzzle performs two slicing operations on top of each other.

First, we take the substring from the second index (position 1) to the sixth index (position 7 - 1) to get `'retsam'`.

We then reverse this string and the result is `master`.

7.3 Built-in Python Operations

```
# Elo 1609

odds = [1, 3, 5, 7]
s = sum(odds) + max(odds) + min(odds)

print(s)
```

What's the output of this code snippet?
Correct: +10 Elo points / Wrong: -10 Elo points

We add three elements together: (1) The sum of the elements of the list, (2) the maximum element of the list, and (3) the minimum of the list.

So, in total, we have: `16 + 7 + 1 = 24`

7.4 Strings and Lists I

```
# Elo 1602

numbers = '1-2-3-4-5-6-7-8-9'

my_list = numbers.split('-')
my_list[::2] = (len(numbers) // 4 + 1) * 'X'

out = ''.join(my_list)
out = out.replace('X', '')

print(out)
```

What's the output of this code snippet?
Correct: +10 Elo points / Wrong: -10 Elo points

This puzzle first creates a string of the numbers 1-9 with a '-' delimiter. Then, we split the numbers on the delimiter to get a list just containing the numbers 1-9.

We change the result using advanced slice assignment notation. Slice assignment is similar to slicing but on the left-hand side of the equation. Using slicing, we select the elements to be replaced with the elements on the right-hand side of the equation. In this case, we replace every other value with 'X'.

Note that the expression on the right-hand side of the equation evaluates to 'XXXXX'. We used the multiplication operator on the string 'X' to create this sequence based on the length of the collection.

If the right-hand side was just 'X', Python would raise a ValueError because you cannot assign a sequence of length 1 to a slice of length 5.

At this point, the variable `my_list` contains a list of strings where every list element with an odd index is equal to 'X'.

We join this sequence on the empty string, resulting in 2468.

7.5 Formatting Printouts

 # Elo 1887

```
print(format(0.1, '.5f'))
```

What's the output of this code snippet?
Correct: +10 Elo points / Wrong: -10 Elo points

This one-liner puzzle dips into Python's syntactic sugar using the format function. Don't worry if you haven't solved it – it's only important that you try, realize your knowledge gap, and fill it immediately.

The format() function takes two arguments: The first argument is the value to be formatted, the second is the formatting specifier and defines how the value should be formatted.

The term '.5f' specifies that the number should contain 5 positions after the decimal point.

Thus, the output is 0.10000.

7.6 Floating Point Comparisons

```
# Elo 1765

a = 0.1 + 0.1 + 0.1
b = 0.3

print(a == b)
```

What's the output of this code snippet?
Correct: +10 Elo points / Wrong: -10 Elo points

7.6. FLOATING POINT COMPARISONS

This puzzle performs a simple arithmetic computation adding together the float value 0.1.

The question seems to be very simple—but as we'll see in a moment, it's not simple at all.

Your inner voice is wrong. And while it is not so important why it's wrong, it is important that you learn to distrust your intuition and your urge to be a lazy thinker. In coding, assuming that things are super-simple is a deadly sin.

In the puzzle, you have assumed that 0.1 represents the decimal value 0.1 or 1/10. This is a natural but incorrect assumption. The value 0.1 doesn't exist in your computer. Instead, your computer stores every number in a binary format consisting only of zeros and ones.

Use an online converter to convert the decimal value 0.1 to a binary value and you will get:
0.000110011001100110011...

The floating point representation of 0.1 in binary has an infinite number of digits. So, your computer does the only thing it can do: limit the number of digits.

This has the following effect. The decimal number 0.1 is represented by the closest floating point number 0.1000000000000000005551115... that can be represented in limited space.

Now, it's easy to see why `0.1 + 0.1 + 0.1 != 0.3` and that the answer is `False`.

As one of our readers, Albrecht, correctly pointed out, the problem can be fixed with Python's `Decimal` module:

```
from decimal import Decimal

a = 0.1 + 0.1 + 0.1
b = 0.3
print(a == b)
# False

c = Decimal('0.1') + Decimal('0.1') + Decimal('0.1')
d = Decimal('0.3')
print(c == d)
# True
```

You can see that the equality of Decimal variables `c` and `d` gives the expected result `True`.

7.7 Python's Multiple Assignment II

 # Elo 1678

7.7. PYTHON'S MULTIPLE ASSIGNMENT II

```
odd = [1, 3, 5]
even = [2, 4, 6]

nums = 6 * [' ']
nums[::2], nums[1::2] = odd, even

print(nums)
```

What's the output of this code snippet?
Correct: +10 Elo points / Wrong: -10 Elo points

CHAPTER 7. PUZZLES: INTERMEDIATE TO PROFESSIONAL

Here, we have two sequences – one with odd and one with even numbers.

Then, we create a list with six white-space characters using simple list arithmetic. The white-space characters serve as *dummy values*, intended only for initializing a list of six elements.

Using a combination of slice assignments and multiple assignments, we replace the elements with even indices by the odd numbers and the elements with odd indices by even numbers.

The result is the sequence [1, 2, 3, 4, 5, 6].

7.8 The Not-So-Obvious Case

```
# Elo 1698

unknown = #input ??
str_ = unknown[0]

if str_ in 'a' and len(unknown) == 1:
    print('X')
```

What's the output of this code snippet?
Correct: +10 Elo points / Wrong: -10 Elo points

This puzzle is a trap.

Seeing all the stuff the puzzle is doing, your brain wants to think about the if branch and what the output would be.

In reality though, the puzzle throws an error. We cannot assign a variable to comment. It's as if there is nothing on the right-hand side of the equation.

So, Python raises a `SyntaxError: invalid syntax`.

7.9 Rounding Values

```
# Elo 1701

b = round(15, -1) == round(25, -1)
print(b)
```

What's the output of this code snippet?
Correct: +10 Elo points / Wrong: -10 Elo points

CHAPTER 7. PUZZLES: INTERMEDIATE TO PROFESSIONAL

If you have to think about the basics, you'll struggle with more advanced concepts that build upon those basics.

Rounding values is certainly one of those basic pieces of wisdom you have to learn.

The **round()** function takes two arguments. The first is the value to be rounded. The second argument is the number of digits to round to. A positive number, say 5, means it will round the number to 5 decimal places. A negative number, say -2, means it will reduce the number of significant digits by 2 e.g. 1234 becomes 1200.

Python then rounds to the next number with the specified precision:

- Value 1.5 is rounded to 2 and value 2.5 is rounded to 2 and so on.

- Value 1.55 is rounded to 1.6 and value 1.65 is rounded to 1.6 and so on

- Value 15 is rounded to 20 and value 25 is rounded to 20 and so on.

Rounding happens as you would expect, unless the last number is 5. Then Python uses "banker's rounding" which means it rounds to the nearest even value as a tiebreaker.

If the second to last digit is odd, Python rounds up. Thus `round(15, -1)` is 20. If the second to last digit is even, Python rounds down and so `round(25, -1)` is 20.

Hence, the result is `True`.

7.10 Initializing Integers

```
# Elo 1761

n = int('1101', 2)
print(n)
```

What's the output of this code snippet?
Correct: +10 Elo points / Wrong: -10 Elo points

This puzzle gives you an interesting new way of initializing integers by using binary values. This is useful if you load some binary values from a file on your computer and you need to convert them.

Specify the string input as the first argument and the base as the second argument. Then, Python does the conversion for you: 1 * 2**3 + 1 * 2**2 + 0 * 2**1 + 1 * 2**0 = 8+4+1 = 13.

7.11 Basic Typing

```
# Elo 1619

type_1 = type(round(1.9, 0))
type_2 = type(round(1.9))

print(type_1 == type_2)
```

What's the output of this code snippet?
Correct: +10 Elo points / Wrong: -10 Elo points

7.12. SHORT CIRCUITING

The built-in `round()` function accepts two parameters:

1. the value you want to round, and
2. the number of digits (precision).

Python is a very intuitive programming language. Rounding is no exception: If you pass a value for the number of digits, the result of `round()` is a float. If you don't, the result is an integer.

Python rounds to the closest multiple of 10 to the power of -*(number of digits)*. So for two digits, we round to the closest multiple of 10^{-2} and for zero digits, we round to the closest multiple of $10^{-0} = 1$ (which are integers).

If two multiples are equally close, it rounds towards the even choice. This is called *banker's rounding*. For example: `round(1.5, 0) = 2.0` and `round(2.5, 0) = 2.0`.

In the puzzle `type_1` is of type `Float` and `type_2` is of type `Int`, so the result is `False`.

7.12 Short Circuiting

```
# Elo 1781

a = 1 > 0
```

```
if a or (1 / 0 == 0):
    print('ok')
else:
    print('nok')
```

What's the output of this code snippet?
Correct: +10 Elo points / Wrong: -10 Elo points

7.12. SHORT CIRCUITING

This puzzle shows you how the optimization of *short-circuiting* works in Python.

Short circuit evaluation in any programming language is the act of not executing unnecessary parts of a Boolean expression.

Say, you want to calculate the result of the expression `A and B` but you already know that `A = False`. Because of your knowledge of the first part of the expression, you know it evaluates to `False`. So the programming language skips computation of the remaining expressions and just returns the result.

In the first line, the expression `1 > 0` gets evaluated and `True` is stored in the variable `a`.

An expression containing `or` evaluates to `True` if one of the operands is `True`. So Python's compiler does not check the second operand of the `or` operation after determining that the first part is `True`.

It's only because of this feature, short-circuiting, that the code actually compiles. Without it, the second part of the `or` expression would raise an error because it is not possible to divide by zero.

Therefore, the result is `ok`.

7.13 While Arithmetic

```
# Elo 1619

n = 16
x = 0

while x < 3:
    n /= 2
    x += 1

print(n)
```

What's the output of this code snippet?
Correct: +10 Elo points / Wrong: -10 Elo points

7.14. THE LAMBDA FUNCTION

The core of this puzzle is the while loop which repeatedly executes the loop body (the indented code block) as long as the loop condition evaluates to `True`. Once the condition evaluates to `False` the loop stops executing.

Inside the while loop we divide `n` by `2` and reassign the result to `n`.

Remember: the result of a division (`/`) is of type float.

In the next step, we increment the value of `x` by `1`. Since `x` is initialized with `0`, the loop is executed three times (`x=0, x=1, x=2`).

Thus, `n` is divided by `2` three times, and the final result is `16 / 2 / 2 / 2 = 2.0`.

7.14 The Lambda Function

```
# Elo 1601

inc = lambda x : x + 1

print(inc(2))
```

What's the output of this code snippet?
Correct: +10 Elo points / Wrong: -10 Elo points

With the keyword `lambda`, you define an anonymous function that is not defined in the namespace.

In contrast to explicitly defined functions, a lambda function does not have to have a specified name. In practice, the lambda function is often used to define a simple function in a single line of code to make it more concise. The syntax is:

`lambda <argument name> : <return expression>`.

In this puzzle, we define a function `inc(x)` which returns the incremented value `x + 1`.

After calling `inc(2)`, the function returns 2 + 1 = 3.

7.15 Zip

```
# Elo 1721

l1 = ['a', 'b', 'c']
l2 = [1, 2, 3]
l3 = []

for tuple in zip(l1, l2):
    l3.append(tuple)

print(len(l3))
```

7.15. ZIP

What's the output of this code snippet?
Correct: +10 Elo points / Wrong: -10 Elo points

To understand how Python's built-in `zip(x, y)` function works, start with your intuition. Visualize a zipper which takes two sides of a jacket and zips them together, one tooth at a time. The `zip` function does the same thing. It takes two lists and zips them together into one single list of tuples which contain the paired elements.

For example, the first element of the first list is paired with the first element of the second list. Similarly, the second element of the first list is paired with the second element of the second list, and so on. In a more code-like way: `[(l1[0], l2[0]), (l1[1], l2[1]), ... ]`.

If the lists are not of equal length, the remaining values of the longer list are omitted.

We zip together the two lists and loop over them. On each loop, we append the element to a new, empty, list. This results in another list which looks like this: `[('a', 1),('b', 2),('c', 3)]`.

The length of this list is `3`.

7.16 Basic Filtering

```
# Elo 1601

list_ = list(range(5))
func = lambda x: x % 2 == 0
ns = []
```

7.16. BASIC FILTERING

```
for n in filter(func, list_):
    ns.append(n)

print(ns)
```

What's the output of this code snippet?
Correct: +10 Elo points / Wrong: -10 Elo points

Using Python's `range(x)` function, the puzzle first creates a list that contains the values 0, 1, 2, 3, 4.

The variable `func` points to a lambda expression.

If you wanted to write the lambda expression as a function, it would look like this:

```
def func(x):
    return x % 2 == 0
```

The function returns `True` for even numbers and `False` for odd numbers.

The built-in function `filter` takes two arguments: `expression` and `container`. The `expression` is a function with 1 argument that returns either `True` or `False`. The `container` is any container type e.g. list, set, dictionary etc.

Filter applies `expression` to every element in `container` and only keeps the elements that return True. In other words, the function "filters" out the False values.

As `func` returns `True` for even numbers, this filter object contains the even numbers from our container.

In the for loop we iterate over the filter object and append its values to the list `ns`.

Thus, `ns` contains all even values form 0 to 4 i.e. [0, 2, 4].

7.17 List Comprehension

 # Elo 1627

```
list_ = list(range(4))
incs = [x + 1 for x in list_]

print(incs)
```

What's the output of this code snippet?
Correct: +10 Elo points / Wrong: -10 Elo points

Much like in the previous puzzle, the variable `list_` is initialized in two steps: first, create a range object with values from 0 to 3 and then convert it to a list using the `list()` function. This gives [0, 1, 2, 3].

Next, we use a powerful Python feature: the *list comprehension*.

List comprehensions are a compact way to create lists. The simple formula is [`expression` + `context`].

- Expression: What to do with each list element?

- Context: Which list elements to select? It consists of an arbitrary number of for and if statements.

For example, the statement [`x for x in range(3)`] creates the list [0, 1, 2].

In the puzzle, we use a list comprehension to increment each element in `'list_'`. The resulting elements are stored in the list `incs`.

Hence `incs` is [1, 2, 3, 4].

7.18 Encryption by Obfuscation

```
# Elo 1821

encrypted = 'Dbftbs!fodszqujpo!jt!opu!tfdvsf"'
```

7.18. ENCRYPTION BY OBFUSCATION

```
decrypted = ''

for c in encrypted:
    decrypted += chr(ord(c) - 1)

print(decrypted)
```

What's the output of this code snippet?
Correct: +10 Elo points / Wrong: -10 Elo points

To decrypt a given message, this puzzle uses two basic Python functions: `chr` and `ord`.

Interestingly, these functions are provided in almost all programming languages (thought sometimes with different names).

The `chr` function returns a character corresponding to the passed ASCII value (for example, the character `'a'` for the ASCII value of 97).

The `ord` function does the opposite; it returns the ASCII value of a given character (e.g. the integer value 65 returns `'A'`).

First, we convert c to its ASCII value using the `ord` function, then we decrement this value by 1. Finally, we convert this back to the corresponding character with the `chr` function.

The end result of our for loop is that each character in the string `'encrypted'` is shifted one letter back in the alphabet i.e. D becomes C[1].

The result is `decrypted: 'Caesar encryption is not secure!'`.

---

[1]This encryption is called *Caesar's cipher* because it was used by Julius Caesar to encrypt his private conversations.

7.19 String Dictionary

```
# Elo 1611

dict_ = {
    0: ' ', 3: 'eat', 2: 'apple',
    4: 's', 1: 'Bob', 5: '.',
}

words = [1, 0, 3, 4, 0, 2, 4, 5]
sentence = ''

for w in words:
    sentence += dict_[w]

print(sentence)
```

What's the output of this code snippet?
Correct: +10 Elo points / Wrong: -10 Elo points

The variable `dict_` has integer keys in the range 0-5 and strings as values.

The list `words` is initialized with keys from `dict_`.

The string `'sentence'` is initialized as an empty string using triple quotes `'''` at both ends (the Pythonic way to write multi-line strings).

After these initialization steps, we iterate over all numbers in `words`. For each number, we look up the corresponding string in `dict_` and concatenate it to `sentence`.

After the loop finishes, `sentence` contains the string `'''Bob eats apples.'''`—which is output of the print statement.

7.20 Functions are Objects

```
# Elo 1641

def add(a, b):
    return a + b

def mult(a, b):
    return a * b

func_dict = {0: add, 1: mult, 2: lambda x: x + 1}

a = func_dict[0](3, -1)
```

7.20. FUNCTIONS ARE OBJECTS

```
b = func_dict[1](4.0, 0.5)

print(a + b)
```

What's the output of this code snippet?
Correct: +10 Elo points / Wrong: -10 Elo points

The puzzle defines two simple functions `add` and `mult`. Each takes two arguments `a` and `b`.

We store the two functions, as well as an anonymous lambda function, in the dictionary `func_dict` with keys 0, 1, and 2 respectively.

Using `func_dict` and bracket notation, we call the `add` function like so `func_dict[0]`. We pass the arguments `3` and `-1` which returns 3 + -1 = 2. This value is stored in variable `a`.

Second, we call the `mult` function using `func_dict[1]` with arguments `4.0` and `0.5`. This returns 2.0 and it's stored in the variable `b`.

Third, we print the sum of `a` and `b` which is 2 + 2.0 = 4.0.

Note that to perform this summation, Python implicitly converts the integer `a` = 2 to a float–that is 2.0. This is because `b` is a float and `int` + `float` = `float`.

Hence, the result is the 4.0 and not 4.

7.21 Dictionary of Dictionaries

```
# Elo 1639

customers = {
    100: {'name': 'Alice', 'zip': 1234},
```

7.21. DICTIONARY OF DICTIONARIES

```
    101: {'name': 'Bob', 'zip': 1212},
    102: {'name': 'Clare', 'zip': 1001},
}

customers[101].clear()

print(len(customers))
```

What's the output of this code snippet?
Correct: +10 Elo points / Wrong: -10 Elo points

In this puzzle, we first define a dictionary `customers`. Each value in `customers` is also a dictionary containing the name and zip-code information of a single customer.

We access the data of customer number `101` using bracket notation `customers[101]` and call the `clear()` function. This removes all key-value pairs in the dictionary `customers[101]`.

So, the key `101` is now mapped to the empty dictionary `{}`.

Finally, we print the length of the dictionary `customers` which is `3`. This is because the number of key-value pairs in `customers` is still `3`. Even though we have cleared the contents of the dictionary, the key `101` still has a value, namely the empty dictionary.

Note that if we had cleared the contents of `customers` instead of `customers[101]`, then the printed output would have been zero.

7.22 Sorting Dictionary Keys

```
# Elo 1667

zip_codes = {
    3001: 'Dolomite',
    3002: 'Goodwater',
    3003: 'Montevallo',
```

7.22. SORTING DICTIONARY KEYS

```
    3004: 'Shelby',
    3000: 'Vance',
}

keys = list(zip_codes.keys())
keys.sort()

print(keys[0])
```

What's the output of this code snippet?
Correct: +10 Elo points / Wrong: -10 Elo points

This puzzle defines a dictionary `zip_codes` with integer keys.

First, we access all keys in the dictionary `zip_codes` using the `keys()` method. Then we cast them into a list using the `list()` function and finally assign them to the variable `keys`.

At this point, the variable `keys` is [3001, 3002, 3003, 3004, 3000].

Second, we rearrange the integers in the list `keys` in ascending order by calling the built-in `sort()` method which can be called on any list object.

Third, we display the smallest of the keys by printing `keys[0]` which is 3000.

7.23 Pythonic Loop Iteration

```
# Elo 1701

prices = [0.55, 0.45, 0.35, 1.45]
items = ['cucumber', 'paprika',
         'tomato', 'broccoli']

item_prices = {}

for key, value in zip(items, prices):
    item_prices[key] = value
```

```
print(item_prices['tomato'])
```

What's the output of this code snippet?
Correct: +10 Elo points / Wrong: -10 Elo points

This puzzle shows you how to build a dictionary from two lists. Here, we use the `zip()` function to loop over the lists `items` and the `prices` together in a single for loop.

On the i-th loop iteration, the variable `key` stores the i-th element in the list `items` whereas the variable `value` stores the i-th element in the list `prices`.

Using these `key` and `value` pairs, we gradually populate the (initially empty) dictionary `item_prices`.

Finally, we print the price of `'tomato'` from the dictionary `item_prices`—which is 0.35.

7.24 Filtering with List Comprehension

```
# Elo 1731

item_prices = [
    ('car', 10000),
    ('boat', 7000),
    ('bike', 400),
    ('skateboard', 150),
    ('aircraft', 500000),
]
```

7.24. FILTERING WITH LIST COMPREHENSION

```
my_list = [x for x in item_prices if x[1] > 9000]

print(len(my_list))
```

What's the output of this code snippet?
Correct: +10 Elo points / Wrong: -10 Elo points

In this puzzle, we are given a list of tuples stored in the variable `item_prices`. As the name suggests, each tuple contains the item name and its price.

After we initialize the list of tuples, we use a list comprehension with an if statement to filter out all those tuples where the item's price is less than or equal to 9000.

The resulting filtered list is stored in the variable `my_list`.

Only two of the items in `item_prices` had a price of greater than 9000 and so the length of `my_list` is 2/

7.25 Aggregating with List Comprehension

```
# Elo 1695

prices = [
    ('banana', 1.5),
    ('apple', 2.0),
    ('bread', 2.0),
    ('milk', 1.0),
    ('fish', 3.5)
]

a = sum([x[1] for x in prices]) / len(prices)
```

7.25. AGGREGATING WITH LIST COMPREHENSION

```
print(a)
```

What's the output of this code snippet?
Correct: +10 Elo points / Wrong: -10 Elo points

In this puzzle, we calculate the average of all prices.

The list `prices` is initialized with 5 tuples of the form `(item_name, price)`. We use a list comprehension to access the price of each item (the second tuple element `x[1]`) and create a list of floats.

Then, we sum all the float values using Python's built-in function `sum()`.

Finally, we divide the result by the length of the list `prices` (which is 5). The resulting float value `2.0` is assigned to variable `a`.

Therefore, the printed output of `a` is `2.0`.

7.26 Maximum of Tuples

```
# Elo 1741

speed = [
    ('car', 100),
    ('boat', 20),
    ('bike', 8),
    ('ski', 7),
    ('aircraft', 650),
]
```

7.26. MAXIMUM OF TUPLES

```
print(max(speed)[1])
```

What's the output of this code snippet?
Correct: +10 Elo points / Wrong: -10 Elo points

This puzzle operates on a list of tuples stored in the variable `speed`. Each tuple consists of a string as the first element and an integer as the second.

By calling the `max()` function on this list of tuples, the tuples are compared to find out which is the maximum.

How can we compare two tuples—and when is a tuple larger than another tuple?

Python compares the tuples `(a,b)` and `(c,d)` by starting with the first elements `a` and `c`. If those are equal (i.e. `a==c`), Python compares the next pair of tuple elements `b` and `d`.

In our case, the first tuple elements are strings. Python compares strings by looking at the Unicode values of the characters from left to right. The tuple with the maximum value is the one with the largest valued string.

The string `'ski'` is the biggest because it starts with the character `'s'` and this is further along in the alphabet than the first letters of the other tuples.

Hence, the expression `max(speed)` returns `('ski', 7)`.

The print statement outputs the second element of this tuple `max(speed)[1]` which is 7.

7.27 The Key Argument

 # Elo 1769

```
speed = [
    ('car', 100),
    ('boat', 20),
    ('bike', 8),
    ('ski', 7),
    ('aircraft', 650),
]

print(max(speed, key=lambda x: x[1])[1])
```

What's the output of this code snippet?
Correct: +10 Elo points / Wrong: -10 Elo points

The previous puzzle was tricky because you may have expected that `max()` returns the vehicle with the highest speed. This is what we accomplish in this puzzle. We show you how to specify the element on which you want to compare two tuples.

We want all comparisons to be based on the second tuple element—that is the speed.

So, we call `max()` with the `key` argument. This specifies a function to apply to each list and the result of this function is used to compare elements.

In this case, we define a lambda function with one argument `x` (a tuple) and the return value of `x[1]` (the second tuple element).

Thus, the second tuple element is the basis of comparison and we compare based on speed and not the string values.

Therefore, `max()` returns (`'aircraft'`, 650) as it has the highest speed value 650.

We print this value 650 via indexing within the print statement.

7.28 Puzzle 123

```
# Elo 1799
```

7.28. PUZZLE 123

```
my_list = ['Hamburger', 'Cheeseburger']

del my_list

print(my_list)
```

What's the output of this code snippet?
Correct: +10 Elo points / Wrong: -10 Elo points

CHAPTER 7. PUZZLES: INTERMEDIATE TO PROFESSIONAL

In this puzzle, we create a new list which we immediately remove from memory using the `del` operation. After this, the list does not exist in memory anymore.

You can use the `del` operation to free some space in memory if you create huge objects which you know you won't need anymore.

As the list does not exist in memory, the puzzle throws a `NameError`.

7.29 Set Operations (1/2)

```
# Elo 1733

set_ = set()

for number in range(100000):
    set_.add(number % 4)

print(len(set_))
```

What's the output of this code snippet?
Correct: +10 Elo points / Wrong: -10 Elo points

7.30. SET OPERATIONS (2/2)

This puzzle gradually populates a set variable named `set_` using a for loop.

The loop repeats `100000` times and the variable `number` takes values from `0` to `99999`.

In each iteration, we apply the modulo operation to `number` using the divisor `4`.

Thus, the result of the modulo operation can only be one of the following `4` values: `0, 1, 2, 3`.

We add this result to the variable `set_` by calling the `add()` method.

A crucial property of the set data type is that it's duplicate-free. In other words, sets do not allow the occurrence of multiple copies of the same value.

Hence, each of the four values returned by the modulo operation can be added to the set only once: on their first occurrence.

Because of this, the length of `set_` is `4` at the end of the for loop—the final result of the puzzle.

7.30 Set Operations (2/2)

```
# Elo 1739

set_1 = {1, 2, 3, 4}
```

```
set_2 = {3, 4, 5, 6}

set_1 = set_1.intersection(set_2)
set_2 = set_2.difference(set_1)

print(len(set_1) + len(set_2))
```

What's the output of this code snippet?
Correct: +10 Elo points / Wrong: -10 Elo points

This puzzle addresses two more set operations that occur frequently in practice.

We define two sets, `set_1` and `set_2`, each of which contains four different values.

Using Python's built-in functions for sets, we calculate the intersection between `set_1` and `set_2` i.e. all elements that exist in both sets.

The result is the set `{3,4}` which we store in the variable `set_1`.

Next, we determine the difference between the newly assigned `set_1` and `set_2`.

The result of this operation is the set `{5, 6}` which we store in the variable `set_2`.

The modified sets both contain two elements.

Therefore, printing the sum of their lengths is `4`.

7.31 Recursive Algorithm

```
# Elo 1899

numbers = [9, 2, 3, 3, 3, 7, 4, 5, 1, 6, 8]

def magic(l):
    if len(l) <= 1:
```

```
        return l
    p = l[0]
    return magic([x for x in l[1:] if x < p]) \
           + [p] \
           + magic([x for x in l[1:] if x >= p])

my_list = magic(numbers)
print(my_list)
```

What's the output of this code snippet?
Correct: +10 Elo points / Wrong: -10 Elo points

7.31. RECURSIVE ALGORITHM

This puzzle provides a recursive implementation of one of the famous sorting algorithms: *Quicksort*.

Quicksort works by repeatedly breaking down the problem (a list of numbers) into smaller chunks (smaller lists of numbers). It then applies Quicksort again on each of those smaller chunks. These are broken down again, and so on until we are left with the trivial case of one element.

We define the function `magic()` to implement the Quicksort algorithm.

The variable `l` represents a list of values.

In our case, `l` is replaced by `numbers` which contains 11 elements.

The first part of `magic` deals with the special case when `l` is empty or contains a single element. IN this case, it returns the list unchanged.

Next, it breaks down `l` into three parts by first determining the dividing position (also called the pivot position) and storing it in the variable `p`.

In our first call, the pivot variable `p` takes the value 9.

The function then returns a list which is a concatenation of three new lists:

1. All values in `l` that are smaller than the pivot value `p`.

2. The pivot value p.

3. All values in l that are greater than (or equal to) the pivot value p.

To obtain the lists of values that are smaller than and greater than p, we use a list comprehension with an *if condition*.

The result is that `magic()` sorts the list `numbers` in ascending order and stores it in the variable `my_list`.

Hence, the output of the print statement is [1, 2, 3, 3, 3, 4, 5, 6, 7, 8, 9].

7.32 Fibonacci

```
# Elo 1809

cache = {}

def fib(n):
    if n < 0:
        raise ValueError

    if n == 1:
        return 0
    elif n == 2:
        return 1
```

7.32. FIBONACCI

```
    if not n in cache:
        cache[n] = fib(n-1) + fib(n-2)

    return cache[n]

fib(10)

print(len(cache))
```

What's the output of this code snippet?
Correct: +10 Elo points / Wrong: -10 Elo points

CHAPTER 7. PUZZLES: INTERMEDIATE TO PROFESSIONAL

In this puzzle, we compute the famous Fibonacci sequence. We use a recursive algorithm with a small but effective optimization (caching).

Each number in the Fibonacci sequence is the sum of the two previous numbers, starting with 0 and 1.

To determine the n-th number in the sequence, the function `fib()` first performs some basic checks: it ensures that `n` is non-negative and that it is not one of the first two numbers.

Then, if `n` is not already determined by a previous `fib()` call, it computes the n-th Fibonacci number.

We achieve this by storing any newly determined Fibonacci numbers in the dictionary `cache`.

Note that `cache` is initialized as an empty dictionary outside of the function. If we initialized an empty dictionary inside the function definition, that would defeat the whole point of caching!

If `n` is not present in the keys of `cache`, it is determined by recursively calling `fib()`. The arguments are `(n-1)` and `(n-2)` and then the returned values are summed together.

The n-th Fibonacci number is stored in `cache` with key `n` for possible future usage.

Note that `cache` is never assigned the Fibonacci values for the values `n = 1` or `n = 2` because their values are

7.32. FIBONACCI

handled by the second and third if statements in `fib()`.

Hence, the call to `fib(10)` will, at most, populate `cache` with keys ranging from 3-10.

Therefore, the length of `cache` after the call `fib(10)` is 8.

— 8 —

Final Remarks

Congratulations, you made it through this whole Python workbook!

By reading this book, you have now acquired a rare and precious skill: speed reading Python code. You have worked through 127 Python puzzles and enhanced your ability to think clearly. Your brain is now wired to solve problems efficiently—one of the most important skills you can have as a software developer (and as a productive person overall).

Your skill level

By now, you should have a fair estimate of your skill level in comparison to others—be sure to check out Table 3.1 again to get the respective rank for your Elo rating. This book is all about pushing you from beginner to intermediate Python coding level. In follow-up books, you'll master the advanced level with harder Python puzzles.

Consistent effort and persistence is the key to success. If you feel that solving code puzzles has advanced your skills, make it a daily habit to solve one Python puzzle a day (and watch the related video on the Finxter.com web app). This habit alone will push your coding skills through the roof—and will ultimately provide you and your family a comfortable living in a highly profitable profession. Build this habit into your life—e.g., use your morning coffee break routine—and you will soon become one of the best programmers you know.

Where to go from here?

I publish a fresh code puzzle every couple of days on our website `https://finxter.com`. All puzzles are available for free. My goal with Finxter is to make learning to code easy, individualized, and accessible.

- I worked hard to make this book as valuable for you as possible. But no book can reach perfection without feedback from early adopters and highly active readers. For any feedback, questions or problems you may have, please send me an email at `admin@finxter.com`.

- I highly appreciate your honest book review on your preferred bookseller (e.g. Amazon or Leanpub). We are not spending tons of money on advertising and rely on loyal Finxters to spread the word. Would you mind leaving a review to share your learning experience with others?

- To grow your Python skills on autopilot, register for the free Python email course here: `https://blog.finxter.com/subscribe`.

- You have now stretched your Python skills beyond intermediate level. There is no reason why you should not start selling your skills in the marketplace right now. If you want to learn how to effectively sell your skills as a Python freelancer, watch the free *"How to Build Your High-Income Skill Python"* webinar at `https://blog.finxter.com/webinar-freelancer/`.

- This is the fourth book in the *Coffee Break Python* series, which is all about pushing you—in your daily coffee break—to an advanced level of Python. Please find the other books below.

Finally, I would like to express my deep gratitude that you have spent your time solving code puzzles and reading this book. Above everything else, I value your time. The ultimate goal of any good textbook should be to *save you time.* By working through this book, you have gained insights about your coding skill level. If you apply your Python skills to the real world, you will experience a positive return on invested time and money. Keep investing in yourself, work on practical projects, and stay active within the Finxter community. This is the best way to continuously improve your Python skills.

More Python Textbooks

This Python workbook extends the "Coffee Break Python" textbook series. It helps you master computer science with a focus on Python coding. The other textbooks are:

Coffee Break Python: 50 Workouts to Kickstart Your Rapid Code Understanding in Python.

The first bestselling book of the "Coffee Break Python" series offers 50 educative code puzzles, 10 tips for efficient learning, 5 Python cheat sheets, and 1 accurate way to measure your coding skills.

Get the ebook:
https://blog.finxter.com/coffee-break-python/

Get the print book:
http://bit.ly/cbpython

Coffee Break NumPy: A Simple Road to Data Science Mastery That Fits Into Your Busy Life.

Coffee Break NumPy is a new step-by-step system to teach you how to learn Python's data science library faster, smarter, and better. Simply solve practical Python NumPy puzzles as you enjoy your morning coffee.

Get the ebook:
https://blog.finxter.com/coffee-break-numpy/

Get the print book:
http://bit.ly/cbnumpy

Coffee Break Python Slicing: 24 Workouts to Master Slicing in Python, Once and for All.

Coffee Break Python Slicing is all about growing your Python expertise—one coffee at a time. The focus is on the important technique: slicing. You use this to access ranges of data from Python objects. Understanding slicing thoroughly is crucial for your success as a Python developer.

As a bonus, you track your Python coding skill level throughout the book.

Get the ebook:
https://blog.finxter.com/coffee-break-python/

Get the print book:
http://bit.ly/cbpslicing

— 9 —

Bonus Chapter: 50 Workouts to Sharpen Your Mind

Are you still hungry for more Python puzzles? Good. I added 50 brand-new bonus puzzles to this second edition of the book. You already know what to do, right? So let's get started!

9.1 Arithmetic

```
# Puzzle 1
x = 5 // -3.0 * 4
print(x)
```

What's the output of this code snippet?
Correct: +10 Elo points / Wrong: -10 Elo points

The result of the previous puzzle is: -8.0.

9.2 Whitespace

```
# Puzzle 2
x = len('py\tpy\n')
print(x)
```

What's the output of this code snippet?
Correct: +10 Elo points / Wrong: -10 Elo points

The result of the previous puzzle is: 6.

9.3 Modulo

```
# Puzzle 3
x = 0
while x < 4:
    x += 1
    if x % 2:
        continue
    print('$', end='')
else:
    print('$', end='')
```

What's the output of this code snippet?
Correct: +10 Elo points / Wrong: -10 Elo points

The result of the previous puzzle is: **$$$**.

9.4 Tuple

```
# Puzzle 4
x = tuple(list('hi'))
print(x)
```

What's the output of this code snippet?
Correct: +10 Elo points / Wrong: -10 Elo points

The result of the previous puzzle is: ('h', 'i').

9.5 Dictionary

```
# Puzzle 5
d = dict([(i, i%3) for i in range(8)])
print(d[5])
```

What's the output of this code snippet?
Correct: +10 Elo points / Wrong: -10 Elo points

The result of the previous puzzle is: 2.

9.6 Asterisk

```
# Puzzle 6
*x, y, z = 1, 2, 3, 4
*x, y = x, y, z
print(x[1])
```

What's the output of this code snippet?
Correct: +10 Elo points / Wrong: -10 Elo points

The result of the previous puzzle is: 3.

9.7 Slicing 1

```
# Puzzle 7
t = [10, 20, 30, 40]
t[100:103] = [10]
print(t)
```

What's the output of this code snippet?
Correct: +10 Elo points / Wrong: -10 Elo points

The result of the previous puzzle is: [10, 20, 30, 40, 10].

9.8 Slicing 2

```
t = [10, 20, 30, 40]
t[2:0] = [10]
print(t)
```

What's the output of this code snippet?
Correct: +10 Elo points / Wrong: -10 Elo points

The result of the previous puzzle is: `[10, 20, 10, 30, 40]`.

9.9 Nested Loop

```
# Puzzle 9
t = [2, 1, 0]
while t:
    k = t.pop(0)
    while t:
        print(k, end='')
        break
```

What's the output of this code snippet?
Correct: +10 Elo points / Wrong: -10 Elo points

The result of the previous puzzle is: **21**.

9.10 List Arithmetic

```
# Puzzle 10
t = [[]] * 2
t[0].append(0)
t[1].append(1)
print(t[0])
```

What's the output of this code snippet?
Correct: +10 Elo points / Wrong: -10 Elo points

The result of the previous puzzle is: [0, 1].

9.11 Exception

```
# Puzzle 11
try:
    x = -9 ** 1/2
    print(x)
except:
    x = 8 * 2 // 5
    print(x)
```

What's the output of this code snippet?
Correct: +10 Elo points / Wrong: -10 Elo points

The result of the previous puzzle is: -4.5.

9.12 Insert

```
# Puzzle 12
t = [3, 4, 5, 6]
t.insert(0, t.pop(t.index(5)))
print(t)
```

What's the output of this code snippet?
Correct: +10 Elo points / Wrong: -10 Elo points

The result of the previous puzzle is: [5, 3, 4, 6].

9.13 Sorted Dictionary

```
# Puzzle 13
d = {'b':1, 'a':3, 'c':2}
print(sorted(d))
```

What's the output of this code snippet?
Correct: +10 Elo points / Wrong: -10 Elo points

The result of the previous puzzle is: ['a', 'b', 'c'].

9.14 Default

```
# Puzzle 14
c = 11
d = 12

def func(a, b, c=1, d=2):
    print(a, b, c, d)

func(10, c, d)
```

What's the output of this code snippet?
Correct: +10 Elo points / Wrong: -10 Elo points

The result of the previous puzzle is: 10, 11, 12, 2.

9.15 Keyword Argument

```
# Puzzle 15
def func(a, b, c=1, d=2):
    print(a, b, c, d)

func(a=1, c=3, d=4, 2)
```

What's the output of this code snippet?
Correct: +10 Elo points / Wrong: -10 Elo points

The result of the previous puzzle is: **error**.

9.16 Global

```
# Puzzle 16
a = 10

def func(x=a):
    global a
    a += 1
    print(x, a)

func(3)
```

What's the output of this code snippet?
Correct: +10 Elo points / Wrong: -10 Elo points

The result of the previous puzzle is: 3, 11.

9.17 Flow 1

```
# Puzzle 17
a = [10]

def func(a):
    a.append(20)
    print(a)

a = [2]
func(a)
```

What's the output of this code snippet?
Correct: +10 Elo points / Wrong: -10 Elo points

The result of the previous puzzle is: [2, 20].

9.18 Flow 2

```
# Puzzle 18
a = 1
b = [10]

def func(a, b):
    a += 1
    b += [1]

func(a, b)
print(a in b)
```

What's the output of this code snippet?
Correct: +10 Elo points / Wrong: -10 Elo points

The result of the previous puzzle is: `True`.

9.19 Enumerate

```
# Puzzle 19
t = {}, {1}, {1,2}, {1:2}
myList = [k for k, v in enumerate(t) \
          if isinstance(v, set)]
print(myList[0])
```

What's the output of this code snippet?
Correct: +10 Elo points / Wrong: -10 Elo points

The result of the previous puzzle is: 1.

9.20 Reverse

```
# Puzzle 20
t = ['world', 'hello', 'python']
sorted_t = t.sort(reverse=True)
print(sorted_t)
```

What's the output of this code snippet?
Correct: +10 Elo points / Wrong: -10 Elo points

The result of the previous puzzle is: None.

9.21 Hierarchical Functions

```
# Puzzle 21
f = lambda x, y: x < y
result = f(f('hi', 'bye'), f(2, 3))
print(result)
```

What's the output of this code snippet?
Correct: +10 Elo points / Wrong: -10 Elo points

The result of the previous puzzle is: True.

9.22 Sorting++

```
# Puzzle 22
d = {3:10, 4:8, 3:9}
print(sorted(d, key=lambda x: d[x], reverse=True))
```

What's the output of this code snippet?
Correct: +10 Elo points / Wrong: -10 Elo points

The result of the previous puzzle is: [3, 4].

9.23 Indexing

```
# Puzzle 23
t = [[1, 2], [3, 4]]
t2 = t * 1
t[0][0] = 10
print(t2[0][0])
```

What's the output of this code snippet?
Correct: +10 Elo points / Wrong: -10 Elo points

The result of the previous puzzle is: 10.

9.24 Count

```
# Puzzle 24
word = 'banana'
print(word.count('ana'))
```

What's the output of this code snippet?
Correct: +10 Elo points / Wrong: -10 Elo points

The result of the previous puzzle is: 1.

9.25 Power

```
# Puzzle 25
x = 2 ** 1 ** 2 % -5
print(x)
```

What's the output of this code snippet?
Correct: +10 Elo points / Wrong: -10 Elo points

The result of the previous puzzle is: -3.

9.26 Lambda

```
# Puzzle 26
t = ['python', 'puzzle', 'fun', 'java']
f = lambda lst: lst.pop(0)
g = lambda lst: lst.pop(1)
h = lambda lst: lst.pop(2)
d = {0:f, 1: g, 2: h}
x = d[f(t) > g(t)](t)
print(x)
```

What's the output of this code snippet?
Correct: +10 Elo points / Wrong: -10 Elo points

The result of the previous puzzle is: `java`.

9.27 Recursion

```
# Puzzle 27
def f(word):
    if len(word) > 3:
        return '*'
    else:
        word += '*'
        return '*' + f(word)

print(f('*'))
```

What's the output of this code snippet?
Correct: +10 Elo points / Wrong: -10 Elo points

The result of the previous puzzle is: ****.

9.28 Kwargs

```
# Puzzle 28
def f(a, b, c, d=4, e=5):
    print(a + b + c + d + e)

args = [10, 20]
kwargs = {'c': 30, 'd': 40}
f(*args, **kwargs)
```

What's the output of this code snippet?
Correct: +10 Elo points / Wrong: -10 Elo points

The result of the previous puzzle is: 105.

9.29 Dictionary Magic

```
# Puzzle 29
def word_dict(word):
    d = {}
    for char in word:
        d[char] = d.get(char, 0) + 1
    return d

x = word_dict('banana')['n']
print(x)
```

What's the output of this code snippet?
Correct: +10 Elo points / Wrong: -10 Elo points

The result of the previous puzzle is: 2.

9.30 Sort Key

```
# Puzzle 30
t = [1, 2, 3, 4, 5]
t.sort(key=lambda x: x % 2)
print(t)
```

What's the output of this code snippet?
Correct: +10 Elo points / Wrong: -10 Elo points

The result of the previous puzzle is: [2, 4, 1, 3, 5].

9.31 Print

```
# Puzzle 31
s = [('hello', 'world'), ('I', 'love', 'python')]
for x in s:
    print(*x, sep='-', end='-')
```

What's the output of this code snippet?
Correct: +10 Elo points / Wrong: -10 Elo points

The result of the previous puzzle is:
`hello-world-I-love-python-`.

9.32 Logic

```
# Puzzle 32
easy = True and False == True and False
print(easy)
```

What's the output of this code snippet?
Correct: +10 Elo points / Wrong: -10 Elo points

The result of the previous puzzle is: `False`.

9.33 Argument Confusion

```
# Puzzle 33
b = 10

def f(a, b=b):
    return a + b

b = 20
print(f(1))
```

What's the output of this code snippet?
Correct: +10 Elo points / Wrong: -10 Elo points

The result of the previous puzzle is: 11.

9.34 Pass

```
# Puzzle 34
for i in range(5, -1, -1):
    if i % 1 == 0:
        pass
    if i % 2 == 0:
        continue
    if i % 3 == 0:
        break
    print(i, end='-')
```

What's the output of this code snippet?
Correct: +10 Elo points / Wrong: -10 Elo points

The result of the previous puzzle is: 5-.

9.35 List Magic

```
# Puzzle 35
t = [1, 2, 3, 4, 5]
t2 = t[:]
count = 0
while True:
    t.insert(0, t.pop())
    count += 1
    if t == t2:
        break
print(count)
```

What's the output of this code snippet?
Correct: +10 Elo points / Wrong: -10 Elo points

The result of the previous puzzle is: 5.

9.36 Zipzip

```
# Puzzle 36
a = [1, 3]
b = [2, 4, 6]
crazy = zip(*zip(a, b))
print(list(crazy))
```

What's the output of this code snippet?
Correct: +10 Elo points / Wrong: -10 Elo points

The result of the previous puzzle is: `[(1, 3), (2, 4)]`.

9.37 Comprehension

```
# Puzzle 37
t = [[i for i in range(j)] for j in range(4)]
print(t[2][1])
```

What's the output of this code snippet?
Correct: +10 Elo points / Wrong: -10 Elo points

The result of the previous puzzle is: 1.

9.38 Slice Extend

```
# Puzzle 38
t = [1, 2, 3]
t.append(t.extend([4, 5]))
print(t[-2:])
```

What's the output of this code snippet?
Correct: +10 Elo points / Wrong: -10 Elo points

The result of the previous puzzle is: [5, None].

9.39 Max

```
# Puzzle 39
t = 'iPhone', 'Italy', '10', '2'
print(max(t))
```

What's the output of this code snippet?
Correct: +10 Elo points / Wrong: -10 Elo points

The result of the previous puzzle is: `iPhone`.

9.40 Zip

```
# Puzzle 40
x = 1, 2
y = list(zip(x))
print(y[0])
```

What's the output of this code snippet?
Correct: +10 Elo points / Wrong: -10 Elo points

The result of the previous puzzle is: (1,).

9.41 Unpack

```
# Puzzle 41
a = [1]
b = [2, 4, 6]
crazy = zip(*zip(a, b))
y = list(crazy)
print(y[0])
```

What's the output of this code snippet?
Correct: +10 Elo points / Wrong: -10 Elo points

The result of the previous puzzle is: (1,).

9.42 Minimax

```
# Puzzle 42
def f(x, y):
    x, y = min(x, y), max(x, y)
    if y % x == 0:
        return x
    else:
        return f(x, y % x)

print(f(16, 72))
```

What's the output of this code snippet?
Correct: +10 Elo points / Wrong: -10 Elo points

The result of the previous puzzle is: 8.

9.43 Sort

```
# Puzzle 43
scores = [100, 84, 63, 97]
scores_sorted = scores.sort()
print(scores[0])
```

What's the output of this code snippet?
Correct: +10 Elo points / Wrong: -10 Elo points

The result of the previous puzzle is: 63.

9.44 Tuple List

```
# Puzzle 44
lst = [(k, k*2) for k in range(4)]
print(len(lst))
```

What's the output of this code snippet?
Correct: +10 Elo points / Wrong: -10 Elo points

The result of the previous puzzle is: 4.

9.45 While

```
# Puzzle 45
i = 2
while i % 3:
    i += 2
    print('!', end='-')
print('!')
```

What's the output of this code snippet?
Correct: +10 Elo points / Wrong: -10 Elo points

The result of the previous puzzle is: `!-!-!`.

9.46 String Logic

```
# Puzzle 46
print('a' and 'b')
```

What's the output of this code snippet?
Correct: +10 Elo points / Wrong: -10 Elo points

The result of the previous puzzle is: **b**.

9.47 Unorthodox Dict

```
# Puzzle 47
pairs = {[1,2]:[2,4,6],
         [10,20]:[20,40,60]}

s = []
for x in pairs:
    s += x

print(len(s))
```

What's the output of this code snippet?
Correct: +10 Elo points / Wrong: -10 Elo points

The result of the previous puzzle is: **error**.

9.48 Count

```
# Puzzle 48
ones = [(1),
        (1,),
        (1,1)]
print(ones.count(1))
```

What's the output of this code snippet?
Correct: +10 Elo points / Wrong: -10 Elo points

The result of the previous puzzle is: 1.

9.49 Cut

```
# Puzzle 49
hair = 100

def cut(times, each=10, hair=hair):
    return (hair - each * times)

hair = 50
hair = cut(2, 20)
print(hair)
```

What's the output of this code snippet?
Correct: +10 Elo points / Wrong: -10 Elo points

The result of the previous puzzle is: 60.

9.50 End

```
# Puzzle 50
if 1 < 2 is True:
    print('nice', end=' ')
if 'A' < 'a' is True:
    print('bravo', end=' ')
else:
    print('great')
```

What's the output of this code snippet?
Correct: +10 Elo points / Wrong: -10 Elo points

9.50. END

The result of the previous puzzle is: **great**.

Printed by Amazon Italia Logistica S.r.l.
Torrazza Piemonte (TO), Italy